food for thought

VANESSA KIMBELL__comes from a long line of female chefs and bakers. Her Italian mother was a senior chef at Keele University and both her English grandmother and Italian great-grandmother were bakers, so it's not surprising that a fourth generation baker of Italian descent would love food.

When Vanessa was nine years old, her parents bought a house in rural south-west France, just 60 yards away from a busy bakery. The bakery supplied all the bread for miles around and was the heart of the community. She fell in love with everything French – the wine, the cheese, the fresh fruit and vegetables, the farmers, and the local markets, but most of all she fell in love with the bread, and spent every spare moment of her childhood working in the village bakery. It was a time that she connected to farmers and the land, and the relationship between food and family and community that was right at the heart of French living. Aged 18, she qualified as a baker and a chef in the UK, but there were no 'real' bakeries. Returning to France, she worked in a restaurant in Paris for a summer and then spent a further year as a baker's apprentice in the Dordogne. Vanessa worked in hotels and restaurants for a further six years, and completed a degree in Psychology of Human Communication. For a number of years she worked outside the food industry, while avidly baking treats for board meetings, but decided to return to her original love of baking and writing once her youngest daughter started nursery. Unsurprisingly, Vanessa's specialist subject is sourdough and baking with wild yeast. She is category leader of the sourdough section of The World Bread Awards and a regular contributor to BBC Radio 4's *Food Programme*. Day to day she teaches sourdough bread making at The Sourdough School in Northamptonshire.

food for thought

CHANGING THE WORLD ONE BITE AT A TIME VANESSA KIMBELL

PHOTOGRAPHY BY LAURA EDWARDS

KYLE BOOKS

DEDICATION__For Mott, for inspiring me;
for Arjen, for challenging me
and for Alastair, for supporting me

First published in Great Britain in 2015 by Kyle Books, an imprint of Kyle Cathie Limited, 192–198 Vauxhall Bridge Road, London SW1V 1DX
general.enquiries@kylebooks.com www.kylebooks.com

10 9 8 7 6 5 4 3 2 1 ISBN: 978 0 85783 271 9

A CIP catalogue record for this title is available from the British Library

Text © Vanessa Kimbell 2015 Photographs © Laura Edwards 2015, except those on the endpapers and page 219 © Vanessa Kimbell and Sean Hawkey
Design © Kyle Books 2015
Editor: Vicky Orchard Copy editor: David Whitehouse
Design: Jane Humphrey Photography: Laura Edwards Food styling: Joss Herd Props Styling: Tabitha Hawkins
Production: Nic Jones and Gemma John

Colour reproduction by ALTA London
Printed and bound in China by C&C Offset Printing Co., Ltd.

MIX
Paper from
responsible sources
FSC® C008047

CONTENTS

FOREWORD__ by Sheila Dillon

One bite at a time, says Vanessa. We can change the world one bite at a time. A bit idealistic? Heard it all before? I mean, hey, what can any one person really do? The thing is…we've been at the changing business for some time. As I was starting to write this, an email popped up with a special offer just for me: 'All-you-can-eat-chicken-wings with a beer' for £15. That's the way we're doing it – one bite, one wing at a time. Billions of us, every day. Screwing our own lives, the planet, and our children's future.

What you've just bought/picked up/borrowed/are thinking about buying is an inspiring book about the part you could play in slowing down our race to global misery. And pulling that off without being worthy and irritating is not easy. No one likes being told what to do. I once asked for salt on my bean sprout and avocado sandwich in a new-agey cafe in California. The waitress looked confused, my sister horrified. My first impulse was to head to the nearest bar for a double bourbon and a cigarette – and I don't even smoke.

Vanessa Kimbell won't drive you to drink – though the Summer Rum Cocktail on page 182 sounds good. What she does in this book, through her honesty and curiosity, is take you with her on her own voyage of understanding that the way we grow, shop, cook and eat shapes our world. With recipes. Recipes that make you want to cook. The world is not short of recipes, we're drowning in them, but these recipes are an addition to anyone's collection. They're simple, they fill you with confidence, they make your mouth water and they work. And by the time you've made Climate Change Shellfish and Lime Paella (page 74), Support Your Local Miller Sourdough Pappardelle (page 123) or While There's Still Time Coffee Frappé (page 174) you've had a tasty education in just how food shapes our lives.

A lot of us who care about food get dismissed as 'foodies'. Though some people wear the label as a badge of honour. It's not. Caring about good food, where it came from, who produced it, how it's grown and what that process did to the soil, the insects, the plants, the birds, the mammals, and the people who worked the land is not 'foodie-ism' – it's being aware of the most basic thing about us and this revolving rock we live on. It's also the most rooted way of understanding power in the world – who has it, who doesn't, who eats well, who can't. Issues for grown-ups, not for people who think that being able to buy a farmhouse cheese is the Saturday morning equivalent of buying a Prada handbag.

Vanessa is not a 'foodie'. She's an enthusiast, a delighter in life's most civilised pleasure, and a grown-up who's retained a child-like wonder at the mysteries and glories of the world. It gives me great pleasure to be able to introduce her and her book to you.

VANESSA KIMBELL__One encounter, one opportunity " So this is how I came to understand that we can all change the world one bite at a time: that the individual and apparently ephemeral decisions we make about the food we buy and eat can, collectively, have a huge impact not just on our own lives, but on people sometimes hundreds or even thousands of miles away. "

ONE ENCOUNTER, ONE OPPORTUNITY Ichi-go ichi-e

I'd bought some Ndali vanilla from a supermarket near where I live, and with my usual inquisitive nature, wanted to find out a little more about what they were doing. So I wrote to Ndali; and out of this came an invitation to see the 2012 harvest at their plantation in western Uganda. I thought that this might make an interesting feature for a radio programme, so, packing my flip flops and tape recorder, I set out for East Africa.

The first things that struck me when I met Ndali's owner, Lulu Sturdy, were the intense blue of her eyes and her smile. Lulu is petite but wiry, with a quiet determination she must have needed when, still in her twenties, she inherited this 800-acre estate near the Rwenzori Mountains. She explained how she had started the Ndali fair trade vanilla company; easy words to write now, but at that point, I hadn't begun to understand what was involved in growing vanilla in Uganda, let alone getting it from there to the UK and on sale in a supermarket. Ndali is like a family to Lulu: she runs the business as their mother. She is nurturing, loving and fair, and she has an instinct, not to do things for people, but to enable them to do the best for themselves. She is strict sometimes and seriously fun at others. Things have not always been straightforward for her, and many of the challenges that she has faced over the past 15 years would have sent most people scurrying back to the safety of the UK. But Lulu is an extraordinary person. I found out just how extraordinary as I went with her, meeting the farmers and finding out more about the production of vanilla.

What I saw was that Lulu had changed lives, not just by encouraging farmers to adopt sustainable methods, but also by creating a structure that meant they were now being paid a fairer price for the crop they cultivated: often two to three times what the free market offered. Formerly, individual farmers were often exploited by middlemen who would pay them the lowest possible price for their vanilla, but as their co-op grew from 50 to 600 and then 1,200 farmers, selling through Ndali at fair trade prices, more of the value could be secured for the local community. It was then that I asked a question that changed my life forever.

> " What, I asked one of the growers, did getting a fair price mean to him? The question was almost a throwaway one. "

He paused for a moment, called his two daughters to him, and replied in a quiet and matter-of-fact way, that a fair price meant that when both his girls were ill he did not have to choose which of them was most likely to survive, because he had enough money to pay for medical treatment for both. I looked down to see two happy smiling children aged perhaps six and ten. They were almost exactly the same age as my own two girls. In that moment my world changed forever. I was completely humbled and the reality of his words left me weak. The price I pay for the vanilla I buy can decide if children on the other side of the world live or die. Nothing has ever been the same since.

I arrived home in turmoil. The people around me were oblivious to the reality that what we choose to buy and eat has consequences. For months I was at a loss about what to do. I felt powerless and angry with the world.

In spring 2013 I was invited to Grenada to meet chocolatier Mott Green. I had first heard of him in 2010, and the man I met was a shrewd 46-year-old New Yorker with a clear vision of what is right, achievable and fair. The combination of Grenada's perfect growing conditions and Mott's inexhaustible energy and ability to get things done had resulted in The Grenada Chocolate Company, making some of the most delicious chocolate you could wish for.

Just to explain: the largest producer of cocoa in the world is an ocean away from Grenada: the Ivory Coast. It's also grown in Ghana, Nigeria and Cameroon, as well as Indonesia and Latin America, mostly on small family farms, and often by some of the poorest people in the world, frequently relying on child labour and sometimes, effectively, slavery. A recent report by the Fairtrade Foundation found that over fifty million people who depend on growing cocoa for their livelihoods, particularly in West Africa, survive on no more than $2 a day, and most cocoa farmers never get a fair price for what they grow. The business model for the majority of the chocolate that we eat means that most of the value from the cocoa trade is attached to the processing of cocoa in the West, and cocoa farmers typically receive just a fraction of the retail price paid by consumers.

Even in Grenada, cocoa farming is still a small and unsophisticated business, as the way cocoa trees grow makes any kind of mechanisation impossible. The difference lies in the business model that Mott Green created, which turned everything on its head. It was more than fair trade: an organic cocoa farmers', processors' and chocolate-makers' cooperative. The beautiful deep burgundy through to banana-yellow pods are grown organically then transported across the river to be fermented; and finally, processed and made into chocolate just a mile from where they were grown. This has made it possible to transfer much of the 'added value' back from multinational processors and retailers to the growers.

It's rare to find people who live by their convictions, and yet Mott managed to draw together others who shared his passion, connecting the chocolate company with a movement called Fair Transport. The Tres Hombres sailing ship under Captain Arjen van der Veen is a beautiful, 32-metre brigantine which uses wind power to carry up to 35 tonnes of cargo over the 6,600km from Grenada to the UK.

The night before the ship left Grenada, with over 50,000 bars from the Grenada Chocolate Company in the hold, it was moored in St Georges Bay, with me on board for a last visit. As one of the crew played a guitar and we sipped rum, I explained my feelings of frustration about

how little power we, as consumers, seemed to have over what happens in the world.

When I asked Arjen and Mott how they had realised their dreams of making the world a better place through fair food and fair transport, Arjen pointed out the obvious: 'This is not how it could be. This is how it is. We are doing it right now. This is my life and it's real.'

Arjen then challenged me. Why did I feel so helpless? What could I do to change things? And something I really wasn't expecting: 'So what are you going to do with your convictions? If you really believe that the world can change, then you just do it. You live it.' In that moment I felt as though I'd been handed the picture of a puzzle I'd long had the pieces for, but with no idea how to put them together. I didn't have a vanilla plantation in Uganda, or a chocolate company in Grenada, or even an ocean-going ship, but I could teach people to make sourdough bread and I could write. I'd found out something about who I was, and realised something I could do. I came home from Grenada a different person: trusting more fully in my beliefs, without questioning, without hesitation. With a new purpose. Seeing this view of the world through other peoples' eyes, I felt that I saw my own place properly. I realised that we can all make a difference.

Thinking back on those feelings: before I started this journey, I felt trapped, in a job I no longer wanted to do, with three young children demanding every ounce of my energy and worrying about the world they were going to grow up in. But I was

> "...a life with principles is at the heart of true happiness. We all have that opportunity: to put the ideas of an ethical and sustainable lifestyle into practice in so many small ways."

expecting someone else to come along and save their world. Now I felt that it was down to me to make my own changes. Sitting around waiting for someone else to make a difference is a miserable way to live. In meeting Lulu, Mott and Arjen, I realised that a life with principles is at the heart of true happiness. We all have that opportunity: to put the ideas of an ethical and sustainable lifestyle into practice in so many small ways, and to incorporate these core values into our daily lives in how to eat, grow and buy food that starts to change the world, one meal at a time.

On 2nd June 2013, only months after I'd met him, Mott Green died. It is with the deepest sadness that I write this. Along with so many of his friends and family, I feel the loss of this utterly extraordinary man, but his words, principles and spirit live on in so many of us. Which brings us back to the Japanese words, Ichi-go ichi-e: one encounter, one opportunity. A lesson that we should cherish every meeting, for the inspiration we may draw from it; because it will never happen in quite the same way again.

BEING SOCIABLE

When you start to think about how to change the way you buy, cook and eat, it is exciting. I, for one, want to share when I find something new, especially if it is food, but trying to be sociable and eat ethically can be a bit tricky. There is a point where discussing rights and wrongs can make people feel judged, and there is a moment when even people you think that you know well can start to feel uncomfortable. My advice when chatting over food is to be prepared to keep the subject light and to talk about how delicious the meal is. I probably avoid talking about the moral values of food, despite the fact that some of the facts surrounding food production are grim, and concern me.

Eating at friends

That said, many people I know love to discuss ethical considerations, and there are lots of positive things that you can do when you are eating at friends. From offering to make one of the courses to buying fair trade wine or local flowers as gifts. I've been known to ask if I could take some leftovers after children's parties to feed to my chickens, or even put an unwanted roast chicken carcass in a bag to take home to make soup with. It's sometimes hard to ask for leftovers, but usually if you explain that it is part of a plan or a resolution to be more green then people are generally obliging.

Local pubs and restaurants

Local pubs often sell a 'guest' or local beer. It's always worth asking for, because aside from usually tasting good, you may be helping to support a smaller business in your own community. Increasingly, independent pubs and restaurants are using local produce and labelling it as such on the menu. Ingredients are the starting point for any good dish and chefs are in a key position to support their local food producers, but that isn't always clearly communicated, so don't be afraid to ask your waiter or waitress what is in season and where something is from.

Entertaining

This is probably my favourite thing. I love that each dish has a story; an anecdote will always make something taste more delicious to me. I can never serve anything with ginger without recalling a moment on a farm in Grenada, when someone casually asked about scorpions, as the farmer hacked the green shoots off some fresh ginger. 'Oh yes', said our host, 'there are lots under the leaves'. Never has the distance back to the truck felt so far in open-toe sandals.

Equally, I love to talk about where the meat comes from, or choosing asparagus at the local farm shop with the people that grew it. Sometimes I will even get my guests to pick the salad out of the garden and wash it as I am preparing a meal, or run out to the hen house to see if there is an extra egg. For me, entertaining is about engaging my guests in the food. If I am lucky my guests have their own stories to share – and talking is part of the joy of both changing and challenging the way we think about our food.

BEING HUMAN

> " Being human is being a lot of things at the same time. "
>
> Matthias Schoenaerts, 1977–

As a travelling writer and baker, I have met some of the people that grow our food, not just in the UK but across the world, in Vietnam, India, Uganda and Grenada. Our own farmers face very challenging circumstances and maybe I now have some insight into what they are dealing with. I also have a young family, three beautiful, bright children with hopes and dreams of their own, and I run a sourdough bakery school. So food not only has to be delicious, for me it also has to be ethical and sustainable. When I first set out to write this book, I wanted to provide some help, in the form of easy recipes, to people navigating the minefield of food 'issues'. It seemed like a simple enough idea.

But the reality is that living ethically and sustainably in a complex world is a huge challenge, and once you start looking at the systems behind the food we eat, it soon becomes clear that we have come to depend on an elaborate and intricate web of compromises and unhealthy solutions. From pesticides, plastic packaging, illegal labour, animal abuse, corporate fraud and additives to the promotion of a convenience food culture which tells us that eating a high-fat, high-sugar diet should become a daily 'treat', our food systems are destroying us and the planet.

About halfway through writing this book I felt I'd lost my way, almost paralysed by the weight of the situation. The more I read and researched, the more I felt that I had embarked on an impossible mission. I'd get tangled up in arguments about which was better – local or organic – or whether the only way to be truly ethical was to become vegan. Who was I to offer a solution? I don't always plan my food; I use diesel fuel to drive to the farmers' market; and who hasn't reached for a ready meal? Yet I still believed with all my heart that we can change the world through food. I had gone from an initial optimism to feeling guilty, under-qualified and overwhelmed. Perhaps, I thought, I should simply admit that I was not able to write this book.

I got further and further behind schedule, until one afternoon my youngest daughter asked me why I was so cross. I explained in the simplest terms about the problems I faced, and that despite my deepest convictions, *I am only human*. She thought for a moment and then said, 'even the best people are not perfect, and nobody knows all the answers, but all you need is to do your best and ask lots of questions… like, what shall I put on my plate? If you write the book then everyone will know to ask questions too, because if the trees are gone and the water is dirty, and there won't be anything left to eat, and no flowers to pick either, what will we do then?'

A child will always point out the obvious.

This isn't a book intended to hector or to tell anyone how to eat. It is book that I hope will open your eyes and get you to question your food choices. I have simply shared some of my recipes, with ideas about how you can make some of your everyday food more sustainable. I had to find the confidence to stand up for my principles. It felt scary, not least because to stick with your own values challenges everything and everyone around you. But at last I came to understand: if you find yourself challenging authority, shout hurrah!

> " This book isn't intended to tell anyone how to eat. It is a book that I hope will open your eyes and get you to question food choices. "

To be a successful food activist, however, you have to make it work in real life, so these recipes are written for busy people: time-poor people who, like me, can't spend all day slaving over a stove or drive for miles to buy a bag of organic carrots. It is a book for real people who don't necessarily want to spend all day in the garden growing vegetables (or even have a garden). I must add at this point that, garden or not, eating ethically should not be the preserve of the well-off. It should not be a privilege to eat good, decent food, but don't fall for the myth that it is a time-consuming thing to do either. The food industry has done a very good job of making us doubt our ability to take control of our own food.

A good example of this is the constant propaganda about giving us the cheapest food, regardless of the ramifications.

Take a supermarket oven-ready chicken for example. So cheap that it begs the question of how exactly does a whole bird cost less than a pint of beer, after paying the poultry farmer and allowing for the retailer's profit margin? Do we know, or think about, the sacrifices that may have been made in animal welfare, in the diet or comfort of the bird, or in how it was slaughtered, and do we really hear the reports that tell us that 70 per cent of supermarket chickens are contaminated on their skin with campylobacter, an organism that can cause serious food poisoning, due to faecal contamination?

No one wants to pay over the odds for their food, but the true cost of cheap food is not to be judged in pounds and pence alone, nor is it without consequences. On the other hand, feeling guilty for being part of this system is not going to change the world; but joy and hope and being empowered might.

I realise that turning the way we are doing things around is a huge task, but each small step, each recipe, each and every ethically produced meal is a step towards a better, brighter future. So what I hope is that this book empowers people to be food activists in the most delicious and practical way possible. I hope that it will result in you, the reader, asking questions. We can only do our best, and I hope the recipes, opinions and stories in this book give you food for thought, and inspiration to change your everyday food for the future of our planet and our children.

PLAN YOUR FOOD

Here's the deal. Most food waste is avoidable. You know it, I know it, but still we put so much food in the bin that the cash value of an average family's food waste is estimated at a staggering £700 each year. Research shows that there are two main reasons why we throw away good food: we cook or prepare too much or we don't use it in time.

So let's assume that making a shopping list for the meals we needed in the coming week would take 10 minutes. That is 520 minutes in a year; less than 8.7 hours. If this little bit of planning enabled a family to avoid putting food in the bin, the saving would work out at over £80 an hour: just for thinking ahead and writing a list.

Actively reducing food waste doesn't just help your wallet but the world around us, too. The environmental impact has been measured and if we stopped food waste, we could prevent carbon dioxide emissions equivalent to taking one in four cars off the road, and save energy, food miles and the clean water that goes into producing wasted food.

Other practical steps you could take include keeping a food-waste diary for a few weeks, so that you learn about what you are throwing away, and maybe understand why (which may help you to break some unhelpful habits); buying in smaller quantities, so less food goes stale; checking the temperature of your fridge, to reduce the amount of food that you think is going off; and if you are into home freezing, do it in smaller packages, so that you then only take out what you need to make a meal later.

Be mindful when you eat

In 2009 I travelled across Vietnam and came home with a new way of thinking. Buddhism had answered so many of my questions that I'd converted. But I was very reticent about attending the local Buddhist Centre. I kept myself busy with thoughts such as 'what if they try to get me to sign anything?'… 'what if they ask me to give up my worldly belongings and be vegetarian or chant?'. It took me almost a year to find the courage to attend. Imagine my surprise to find that the people were… wait for it… normal. Yes normal. They were not wearing funny clothes, they had everyday jobs and did not ask me to do much at all, other than consider the world, the kindness in it and my place in that kindness.

Meditation seemed to click with me from the start, as I contemplated the 'Kindness of Others' from the *Eight Steps to Happiness* by Geshe Kelsang Gyatso. In this, he wrote: 'Through receiving a constant supply of food, drink, and care, our body gradually grew from that of a tiny helpless baby to the body we have now. All this nourishment was directly or indirectly provided by countless living beings. Every cell of our body is therefore the result of others' kindness.'

That is what I try to connect to, in practising mindfulness when I eat. I try to hold onto the moment, being there in that second, and I try to taste that kindness. The farmers that grew the vegetables or harvested the grain, the tea picker who picked the tea, the designer who thought up the packet that the food arrived in, the lumberjack that cut the wood to make the box, the worker in the factory that processed the food, the driver that transported the food, the person that designed the oven that I cook my food in. We are all connected.

There is no them and us. The simplest of meals can connect us to every continent: coffee from Africa, spices from India, bananas from the Caribbean or Latin America. We are one world, one air, one water, one planet.

I'm not for one moment saying that to be ethical in your everyday food and cooking you need to practise Buddhism. But cultivating a focused awareness of the present moment and contemplating the efforts of others that got your food to your plate is a good thing to do. I don't claim to be 'mindful' with every mouthful. Like most people, my life is busy and I am often at full stretch, but when I stop and take a moment to consider my food, it tastes. I mean really *tastes*. In that mouthful the world can stand almost still. The clock ticks, I can feel my breath and I am connected to my food, and the people that grew it.

"Food is our common ground, a universal experience." James Beard, 1903–1985

GROW YOUR OWN HERBS

Aged 18 and freshly qualified as a baker, I worked nights in a local bakery in the Dordogne. My bright-eyed French beau would save for weeks to treat me to a meal in a wonderful restaurant called Z'haricot vert (The green bean) and we immediately made friends with the chef, Jean Bernard Lavaud. Bernard's kitchen was a delight. Ingredients were chosen with care when he'd visit the local market and meet the farmers, and the day he showed me the small herb garden at the back of his kitchen changed they way I cooked forever. The only herb I'd encountered in catering college was a limp sprig of parsley used as garnish, or perhaps in some white sauce for fish.

> **"Nothing beats herbs picked straight from the garden, but some are not available fresh all year round so freshly dried herbs can concentrate the oils and capture the flavour."**

I was smitten. Common herbs are found in most gardens, but there are many more unusual varieties that really can bring a huge array of new tastes to everyday cooking. By comparison, buying a packet of basil that has lost most of its flavour and aroma while being flown thousands of miles, just to make fresh pesto in midwinter, is both uneconomical and environmental stupidity. But the best advice I can give is only grow what you are likely to use or able to share. Herbs are essentially wild plants, and cutting them for the kitchen only keeps them in check until the new growth is stimulated. And when it comes to using herbs, the only limit is your own imagination: for example, one of the easiest things you can do to make your everyday bread more interesting is to incorporate herbs. Stirring a ripple of fresh homemade pesto into a beautiful sourdough loaf gives a superb flavour: one of my favourite kitchen suppers, served with a tomato soup.

So here is my beginner's guide to growing and preserving some of the herbs you can use all year round.

What I really love about herbs is that they are happy to grow in pots. I had no garden for the best part of five years so I had a mobile pot collection outside my back door. It was then that I discovered that herbs actually make great houseplants – they just need a sunny window.

A *bay tree* is wonderful. You don't have to start with a big one – a little plant in a pot will produce enough leaves to keep most families well supplied.

Rosemary is indispensable. It loves being in a pot in a sunny spot.

Lemon thyme grows in the most inhospitable places. It loves the sun and livens up even the most mundane of stews.

Parsley grows well even in winter and there have been many occasions when I've made parsley pesto with leaves picked from the garden on the darkest winter day.

Of course you can't have every herb fresh all year round, so learning to store your herbs correctly gives you a wide range of wonderful options later in the year when you are most in need of kitchen inspiration. It's not just dried herbs that work; frozen herbs or herbs preserved in oil can also be wonderful.

For me, it's essential to grow herbs if you care about flavour or the environment, and anyway, buying herbs every week at the supermarket is expensive. So with very little time and effort you can save yourself money, cook delicious food and help the bees, the butterflies and the birds.

When you harvest herbs from the garden, try to do it around midday on a hot sunny day when the plants are dry, because the heat concentrates the oils for more intensity and wet herbs are more prone to rot when stored. Herbs used for their leaves are best picked before they flower (i.e. as soon as the buds arrive); this will ensure the best flavour because they contain the maximum amount of volatile oils prior to blossoming. Use a pair of strong scissors or a kitchen knife to snip the herbs, and cut herbs used for drying with good long stems.

It is important to wash dirty herbs carefully, then wipe and pat them dry with kitchen paper.

Drying

Herbs can be dried in various ways, but I prefer to do it slowly by hanging them upside down. Remove the lower leaves from the stems and tie them in bunches of no more than 10–12 stalks to allow air to circulate, looping strong thread or very fine cord around the cut end of each little bundle. Find a dry, warm (not humid), dark and well-ventilated place that is out of the way. Attics, pantries and warm basements make ideal spots for drying herbs. The ideal temperature for drying is about 20°C. If you do not have a dark spot in the house, you can try tying a paper bag over each bunch and piercing it with airholes, which has the added bonus of keeping the dust off.

Leave your herbs to dry for 1–3 weeks. Check them every now and then to see how they are drying. You can expect that the thicker-stemmed herbs will take longer. When the consistency is crumbly they are ready. Remove the leaves and store them in airtight glass jars, making sure that you pick out any foreign material that's been caught on the plant. You can keep the leaves whole for making herbal infusions or crush them in your fingers to make a really fine ground mix. Remember to label each storage jar and date it. I only store the herbs for up to one year. Do keep them in the dark to keep the intensity of the colour.

If you want to collect seeds, wait until the blooms have died and the seed heads have set, but do make sure that you get to them before the birds or the windy weather. Pick the heads on short stems and put them upside down into a paper bag, which the seeds will drop into as they dry. Store them whole in a clean jar, only crushing them as they are needed for cooking.

Freezing

Some herbs, such as chives, can only be frozen as they don't dry well. Freezing also works well for soft-leaf herbs such as basil, tarragon, lovage and parsley. Wash and completely dry freshly picked herbs, as left. Next, strip the leaves off and place them into freezer bags or containers. Label and date them as they should really only be kept for up to three months. Or you can freeze herbs in butter in ice-cube trays; they are really handy little sizes for cooking use. If you choose to freeze in water, then freeze approximately one third chopped herbs to two thirds cooled, boiled water. I prefer my herbs to be frozen in butter as they retain more flavour.

Basil is truly wonderful puréed with olive oil before freezing in ice cube trays (do not add water). Store herbs frozen as ice cubes in plastic freezer bags, then use as needed. (Please note that frozen herbs will not work as a garnish – they're only good for cooking.)

Preserving in oil

Harvest, clean and dry herbs as described above, keeping the leaves on the stems. Choose an oil; I like rapeseed, olive and sunflower but any oil you like is generally fine. Place the herb stems in a dry, sterilised bottle, then fill completely with oil, making sure the stems are entirely submerged.

It is important to keep herby oils in the fridge, especially during the summer, because the herbs will deteriorate as the oil warms up, and use within three months. This method is more effective for creating flavoured oils, which will absorb the essence of the herbs stored in them, than as a simple method of preserving the herbs themselves.

Using

If you need to substitute dried herbs for fresh in a recipe, remember that dried herbs are more potent. As a rule of thumb, 1 teaspoon of dried equals 1 tablespoon of fresh. Don't overdo the addition of dried herbs – too much can overpower a dish.

(Opposite) Homemade Free-range Rapeseed Mayonnaise flavoured with herbs
(see page 210)

GROW YOUR OWN HERBS__ **For flavour and aroma in everyday dishes, plant herbs all over the garden.** Lemon thyme along the paths, sage under the roses, fennel at the back of the borders, and bay trees in pots. I scatter dill seeds randomly, let chives grow in the cracks and countenance the rosemary getting a little out of control.

GROW YOUR OWN SALAD

I believe that it is a revolutionary act to grow your own food. Start small. Grow something you can eat. It's one of the most powerful things you can do to change the world for the better.

It's incredible that the average carbon dioxide emissions each year for someone in the West are anything from 5.6 tonnes (France) to over 17 tonnes (USA). One of the major contributors is the transport sector, and food miles play their part in that, so growing your own salad is one small way to reduce your carbon footprint. Another good reason to 'grow your own' is that ready-to-eat salads are often washed in water containing powdered or liquid fruit acids or high levels of chlorine meant to destroy bacteria and microorganisms which can cause food poisoning, such as salmonella, E. coli and cryptosporidium. But this can reduce the nutritional value of the food without always killing the bugs, because if the contamination came from the crop's water supply, the bacteria may still be present inside the vegetables when they are eaten, or – like cryptosporidium – the organisms may not be destroyed by chlorination. Despite this, millions of people are still buying bagged salad in this way.

If the idea of growing your own worries you, then it is worth bearing in mind what an old gardener once told me: 'seeds want to grow'. This always gives me confidence.

My first ever garden was a pot garden. In fact, it was an anything-you-can-keep-soil-in garden. I was watching every penny and rescued some discarded animal feeding troughs, an old Belfast sink and some vegetable oil containers from the back of the Indian takeaway next door. I tenderly planted my first seeds, and they grew, and so began a lifelong love of wandering out of my back door and plucking young, fresh, crispy salad moments before I needed it. Even when I moved to a flat with no garden, I kept pots on the steps. Growing even a small amount in the most impossible place still felt good. The other thing about growing your own is the amount of money you can save. I'm not suggesting that gardening is cheap, but a packet of mixed seeds with a cut-and-come-again crop can keep you in salad for months. In fact, a pack of 500 seeds will cost you about the same price as one 80g bag of supermarket ready-washed salad.

What to grow

Don't think of salad as just a large green supermarket lettuce. There are hundreds of varieties to grow, with wonderful flavours and colours. Red leaves, crunchy leaves, jagged leaves, curly leaves, tiny pungent leaves, big blowsy open leaves, dark green, light green, purple and white. A great place to start is by mixing up the seeds of assorted salad leaves with mustard greens in a jam jar, and then sewing them together to create a patch of mixed salads.

Some of my favourite salad varieties are kale, chicory, coriander, chard, corn salad, endive, land cress, leaf celery, lettuce, mizuna, mustard, pak choi, parsley, radicchio, red rocket, sorrel and spinach. And root crops like beetroot, radish and turnip also have leaves that are really delicious when harvested young.

How to grow your own salad

Good salad starts with somewhere to grow it and good soil. If you have the chance to clear a patch of ground in late autumn or early winter and add well-rotted manure to it, you will be off to a really great start the following year.

Then, from spring onwards, you can rake the soil well, so it is fine. Press a broom handle (with the broom head removed) into the soil to make a 2cm straight drill in the soil and water along it lightly. Mix your seeds with a large tablespoon of either dried sifted earth (you can dry it out in the airing cupboard) or dry sand. This will give you a better, more even, distribution of seeds as they can be tiny. Do check your packet for how many seeds it contains, as most packets will give you enough seeds for several rows of plants, or successive plantings at one to two-week intervals.

Sow your seeds, gently rake a thin covering of soil over them and make sure that you have labelled the rows. Salad crops need plenty of water as they grow, so if rain is scarce, make sure to soak the soil around lettuces on a regular basis, from when the hearts begin to form.

Use a net to stop birds from eating your seedlings and pick off any snails or slugs – I find the best time to do this is at night with a torch.

Harvest your salad as needed, by snipping handfuls of leaves from the plant, about 2.5cm above the crown so it sprouts again, or by cutting the entire 'head'. It tastes so good eaten straight away.

THE DOMESTIC CHICKEN__If you have the space, then keeping chickens is a great way to connect you to your food.
Three chickens are probably enough to supply an average family with eggs all year round, although most hens slow down their laying in the winter.

Our chickens are hilarious; they chase bugs, chase each other and cluck with pride whenever they have laid an egg. They are real characters. I am always sad when I see chickens reared in unpleasant conditions. Even free-range and organic chickens are allocated relatively small areas per bird in commercial production. Chickens kept at home, with the opportunity to live their life outside, are far happier: but do note that they need a degree of protection, as town and country foxes or birds of prey will take the opportunity to have your garden fowl for lunch. The eggs are wonderful! From the joy of collecting them, still warm in the morning, through to cracking them open and finding that the yolks are darker and more intense in colour than supermarket eggs, with a distinctive domed uprightness, while the white has a fresh firmness.

Once your garden flock is established, daily chicken care takes little time. Chickens need food, clean shelter and exercise, but your biggest investment is in buying or building a coop and preparing a safe space for your flock to live. After that, it may take just 10 minutes a day to check that they have plenty of food and water and collect their eggs. We really love throwing scraps for them to snack on and we clean the coop about every three weeks. Last, but by no means least, is the fact that chicken manure makes excellent fertiliser for the garden.

VINTAGE__**We live in a society that throws things away.** *A consumerist society, and one in which the economy is driven by growth; in other words people spending money.* We are constantly being bombarded with messages to buy this, or feel good with a new that, but new is not always the most environmentally friendly choice. In some ways the recession of the past few years has seen a resurgence in make do and mend. For me, there is joy in seeing a tablecloth darned or a bag stitched. I've always been drawn to objects with a past. I know that inanimate objects do not have feelings, but I like to think that if they did they would be delighted to find themselves belonging in a home where they are appreciated. An old saucer, a china teapot or an old chopping board with years of bread slices scored into the wood – I love and treasure old things, but above all else I use them. Vintage items shouldn't just sit on a shelf gathering dust.

Aside from not really liking new things I'm always slightly shocked at their price compared to vintage, and vintage is the ultimate ethical way to shop for most things. It forgives the odd chip, adores the slightly faded, embraces the frayed and celebrates the imperfections. Life is not perfect. (Perhaps that is why I love mismatched things so much.) But my style is about living in the most ethical and sustainable way, and it is more than just the food that I eat – it goes beyond the table. It is everything from the plates you eat off and the washing-up liquid you wash up with to the bags you carry your shopping home in.

SIMPLE SUPPERS

DUMP THE DIET FOOD
PHO GA VIETNAMESE NOODLE SOUP

If you were an alien that dropped in on planet Earth, many things would seem totally crazy. On our TV, we are courted by softly-spoken, sexy 'food porn' adverts, showing sumptuous ready meals packed with calories and desserts dribbling chocolate or baked in all-butter pastry, while the same ad break also insists you eat a healthy range of calorie-controlled ready meals to slim down. They know exactly what they are doing, because one way or another, they tempt you to buy a ready meal. The marketing is designed specifically to make you feel less capable of preparing your own food, as the images offer to take all the strain away by 'empowering' you to pick up a packet and throw it in the microwave. It's about profit for them and certainly not about your health.

I'm not exactly the world's best dieter. In fact, I loathe the very idea, but whenever I feel the need to shift a few pounds I turn to Pho Ga.

I first learnt to cook this recipe in the kitchen of an overnight train as it took us from north to south Vietnam. It was amazing to be in the tiniest of kitchens with the most limited facilities and the humblest chef I ever met, but the focus was on fresh local food as the core of this meal: all the ingredients had been bought that morning at the local market. This dish is gently spiced, warm, comforting, hugely aromatic, wonderfully filling and yet still manages to be fantastically healthy, and I promise it takes almost no effort at all.

SERVES » 4–6

For the stock

30g fresh root ginger, in one piece and unpeeled

2 medium onions, unpeeled

vegetable oil, if you are frying

6 skinless chicken thighs

1.5 litres hot chicken stock

2 star anise

For the soup

salt, to taste

3 tablespoons fish sauce, plus extra to serve

240–300g rice noodles, cooked and refreshed in cold water (60g per serving)

To serve

8 spring onions, cut into rings

400g fresh bean spouts

1 red or green chilli, sliced into rings, plus extra to serve

juice of 2 limes, plus thin-cut lime wedges, to serve

a good handful of herb leaves, such as mint, coriander and basil

Cut the ginger in two, so you have a 'flesh' side and a 'peel' side, and halve the onions, leaving their skin on. Using a heatproof kitchen fork, char them on both sides over a gas flame (or on a griddle). If you prefer, you can roast the onions until slightly burnt, or using a small amount of oil fry the onion and ginger really well before transferring to a large pan. Add the chicken, stock and star anise to the pan. Simmer for about 1 hour until the chicken is really soft. Strain the broth into a bowl, discarding the ginger, onion and star anise, and remove the chicken from the bones keeping the meat to one side.

Return the broth to the pan and bring it back to simmering point. Season with salt and fish sauce. Put the noodles into a sieve or steamer basket and lower them into the broth to reheat for just a few minutes until piping hot.

Share out the noodles between large, deep bowls and top with some chicken meat, the spring onions, bean sprouts, chilli and lime juice. Ladle over the stock. Add the herb leaves and serve with extra fish sauce, chillies and lime wedges.

(*Opposite*) Cultivated Mushrooms on Sourdough Toast (*see recipe page 34*)

CULTIVATED MUSHROOMS ON SOURDOUGH TOAST

I've been quietly picking wild mushrooms in the Dordogne all my life. The best spots for finding them are closely guarded secrets, and woe betide you getting caught by a farmer with a basket full of his girolles! If you're very careful, mushroom picking need only modestly affect the forest ecosystem. Ideally, you leave the foot of the mushroom intact and the mycelium below ground undisturbed, allowing it to re-fruit; you take less than half of what you find and leave the smaller mushrooms to mature; and so you get to pick more another day.

However, there are areas in both the UK and across Europe where wild funghi have been so aggressively harvested that bans on foraging have had to be introduced, and places like Epping Forest where it is simply illegal to take the mushrooms. In some cases forest rangers have carried out spot checks on visitors during the mushroom season, and pickers have been prosecuted. Conservation staff warn that large-scale wild mushroom foraging operations for commercial sale are wrecking some of our oldest and most precious woodlands and putting rare species of funghi at risk.

I don't want to eat unethically foraged ingredients. But there is an alternative: here in Britain, we have specialist growers of 'exotic' mushrooms which can't be called 'wild' simply because they have been carefully cultivated. As the flavour and texture of a mushroom will chiefly be characteristics of its variety rather than specific to where it's grown, I'm happy with that. It may mean that I'm eating locally grown oyster and shiitake mushrooms, rather than the penny bun or common morel. To me they are equally delicious and much less likely to cause an argument.

SERVES » 4

800g 'exotic' mushrooms
2 garlic cloves, crushed and finely
  chopped
120g unsalted butter
4 sprigs of fresh tarragon, finely chopped
sea salt and freshly ground black pepper
4 slices of sourdough bread
200g soft goat's cheese

First prepare the mushrooms. Trim the ends with a sharp knife, brush off any debris or bits of soil and slice them if they're big, so you're left with bite-sized pieces.

Preheat the oven to 180°C/160°C fan/gas 4. Put the garlic into a bowl with the butter, tarragon and a generous amount of salt and black pepper and mix well.

Spread one side of each slice of bread with some of the garlic butter and put on a baking tray. There will be quite a lot of butter left over,

which you will need for the mushrooms. Bake the bread in the oven for 6–8 minutes then arrange on serving plates when the mushrooms are ready.

Meanwhile, put a large frying pan over a high heat. Add the remaining garlic butter and the mushrooms. Sauté the mushrooms, stirring often, for 4–5 minutes until golden. Add the goat's cheese then stir for another minute until it melds into the mushroom mixture. Quickly spoon the mushrooms over the slices of sourdough bread and serve immediately.

RUBBER GLOVES NETTLE SOUP

Growing wild in our woodlands, parks and sometimes even our gardens are nettles, those weeds with hairs that sting your skin. But if more people only knew how delicious and nutritious nettles are, they'd be overjoyed each spring when they found them appearing in unexpected places.

If you compare the taste of nettles to spinach, they are remarkably similar. However, unlike commercially produced spinach, nettles won't have been sprayed with fertilisers or pesticides. If you find them on verges, commons or in public woodlands, it is possible that local councils will have doused them with weedkiller by the summer, so pick them early from anywhere like that to avoid contamination.

Nettles are packed full of goodness, rich in vitamins A and C as well as minerals such as calcium, iron, manganese and potassium, and can be a good source of vegetable protein. Apart from soup, you can also use them in homemade pesto, as a purée or to make a herbal tea (from the dried leaves and flowers). As a folk medicine, the leaves were used to treat kidney and urinary problems as well as arthritis and rheumatism, and in shampoo, nettles are said to make the hair glossy and dandruff-free. But even though they are a free source of food and one which regrows quite quickly, don't be greedy and don't strip an area of its plants: nettles are an important food source for butterflies, including the Small Tortoiseshell and Peacock, as well as moths and the aphids which are a food source for ladybirds.

So pull on your wellies, grab a plastic bag and a pair of scissors, and most of all, find a pair of rubber gloves to protect your hands; because foraging is a wonderful way to connect with the planet you are part of and it is also – providing you don't sting yourself – great fun. And in case you wondered: soaking nettles in water or cooking them destroys the sting.

SERVES » 4–6

200g nettle tops
30ml rapeseed oil
2 medium onions, finely chopped
2 leeks, trimmed, washed and
    finely sliced
2 bay leaves
2 garlic cloves, finely chopped
2 large potatoes, peeled and diced
1.5 litres hot vegetable or chicken stock
salt and freshly ground black pepper
6 heaped tablespoons soured cream
finely chopped mint, to garnish
toasted sourdough bread, to serve

With your rubber gloves on, carefully pick through the nettles, rinsing them thoroughly. Discard any tough stalks, pulling off and keeping just the leaves and the more tender young tips.

Heat the oil in a deep, heavy-based pan over a medium heat, add the onions, leeks, bay leaves and garlic and sauté until soft.

Add the potatoes and stock. Cover and simmer for 14 minutes. Add the nettles, cover and simmer for a further 3 minutes or until the potatoes are cooked and the nettles are tender. You can adjust the thickness by adding a small amount of water if necessary. Season with salt and black pepper.

Purée the soup and check the seasoning. Serve warm, topped with a dollop of soured cream and a good sprinkling of mint, some more black pepper and a large slice of toasted sourdough bread.

FAR-SIGHTED SWEET POTATO AND DILL SOUP

Being ethical and sustainable is never just black and white.

This fragrant, slightly sweet and warming vegan-friendly soup is based on one my Canadian sister-in-law cooks. It's easy to make and just the kind of soup you need to keep you going on a blustery winter's day. The sweet potatoes in my local shop are imported, of course, but I found that with a lot of determination and care I could actually grow them in my garden here in Northamptonshire. They were tiny and a lot of effort, as I had to protect them from the frost, but tasted delicious and they travelled just 20 feet to my kitchen in a bucket. However, I'm not yet convinced that this was a practical thing to do, when there are alternatives worth considering.

Sweet potatoes are a remarkable food source; originally from Latin America, where they have been cultivated for thousands of years, they spread first through Polynesia, long before the arrival of Europeans, and then to New Zealand, the Philippines and by 1600AD to China. In fact, they will grow in any tropical or warm temperate climate, and are a key crop in southwest India, Africa and the southeastern USA.

In northern Senegal, for example, the Diama Dam project a few kilometres from the old colonial city of Saint-Louis had already spanned the Senegal river, with the twin objectives of preventing saltwater intrusion from the nearby estuary and providing a more secure supply of fresh water for the irrigation of semi-arid land. One project running since 2006 has harnessed this to create a farming venture which grows sweet potatoes, chillies, onions, sweetcorn and more. Replacing animal herding and fishing with horticulture has provided new employment opportunities for young people who would previously have drifted to African cities or even towards Europe as economic migrants; and some of the proceeds from exports have gone into providing schools, medical centres and clean drinking water.

This is far-sighted in two ways: local society is stabilised and sweet potatoes have become part of their diet, providing not just carbohydrates and fibre, but also beta-carotene, a precursor of vitamin A, which is important for good vision and eye health, reducing the incidence of cataracts and age-related macular degeneration. The leaves also provide lutein and xanthine, which protect the eyes and may also have wider health benefits. I realise that there are food miles to consider when buying produce imported from Africa, but on balance, I feel that I can use my garden more productively to grow something else for my kitchen, and that a relatively short journey by boat, for Senegalese sweet potatoes which have so many benefits, is a compromise I am willing to make.

SERVES » 6

3 tablespoons coconut oil

3 bay leaves

1 large onion, diced

4 garlic cloves, chopped

1kg sweet potatoes, peeled diced

1kg potatoes, peeled and diced

2 litres hot vegetable stock

a large handful of fresh dill

salt and freshly ground black pepper

crusty bread, to serve

Put the coconut oil in a deep pan, add the bay leaves, onion and garlic and sauté lightly. Add the sweet potatoes, potatoes and stock and stir well. Cover and simmer for 18–20 minutes. Check that the potatoes are cooked and remove the bay leaves.

Chop the dill and add half to the pan. Set half the soup aside and liquidise the other half. Mix the two halves back together in the pan to give you a smooth, thick base with chunks. Stir in the remaining dill and season with salt and black pepper. You can adjust the thickness by adding a little water and heat again if needed. Serve with warm crusty bread.

FINISH-THE-BOTTLE WINE RISOTTO

Most people buy their wine in the supermarket. It's often cheap, even though at least 99 per cent of it has been imported, creating a huge carbon footprint. You can be a more 'aware' imbiber by buying locally made wines or by trying to apply other ethical ideas to your purchases (at least one UK supermarket currently enables you to search specifically for fair trade, vegan, vegetarian and organic wines on its website).

My parents run a small vineyard in Northamptonshire, and this has given me an insider's perspective on the work put in by independent wine producers. Every year our family and friends get together to pick grapes. You could almost be in the South of France, but the grapes are grown just a few miles east of the M1 and the accents are resolutely British. As we pick, we laugh and catch up with what everyone's been doing, but nevertheless we work hard. Throughout the year, my parents prune the vines, shape them by hand, mow and mulch them as needed: all in order to produce perfect bunches of grapes. They are slightly obsessed with producing the most delicious and sustainable wine possible, and though I'm biased, it is wonderful wine. Knowing that it takes 4–5 bunches of grapes to make each bottle really makes me appreciate the effort that goes into every glass, and I don't want to waste it.

So when you end up with an inch or two left over in a bottle, and you are not in the mood to finish it or when it is a few days old, and there's a temptation to tip it down the sink, think twice. You can freeze your leftovers (pour them into a spare ice-cube tray, then store the cubes in a resealable bag), and use them later in this recipe.

SERVES » 4–6

600ml hot organic chicken stock
    (page 208)
2 bay leaves
60g unsalted butter
2 tablespoons rapeseed oil, plus extra
    to serve
3 small leeks, washed and
    finely chopped
3 sprigs of lemon thyme
200g Arborio rice
250ml white or rosé wine
150g baby broad beans
1 heaped tablespoon full-fat
    crème fraîche
salt and freshly ground black pepper
a big handful of grated Parmesan-style
    cheese, plus extra to serve
fresh mint, to serve
2 heaped tablespoons za'atar (optional)

Put the chicken stock into a saucepan, add the bay leaves and bring to a simmer. Meanwhile, in a separate large pan, melt a knob of the butter with the oil and add the leeks and thyme. Cook over a gentle heat until soft and translucent. Stir in the rice and make sure it is thoroughly coated in the butter and oil. Pour in the wine and increase the heat. Bring to the boil, then reduce the heat to a brisk simmer, stirring often, until half the liquid has evaporated.

Add the broad beans with one ladleful of the hot stock. Keep stirring and cook until all the liquid has been absorbed. Then add another ladleful of stock and repeat, stirring constantly. Continue with the remaining stock (topped up with boiling water, if needed) until the rice is cooked but still has a slightly firm texture –

what the Italians refer to as 'al dente' – with a creamy consistency. This takes about 20 minutes. Add the stock gradually so you're not left with a soup at the end, and don't overcook the rice as it will continue to cook for a few minutes when it is removed from the heat.

When the rice is cooked, stir in the crème fraîche. Season with salt and black pepper to taste, cover and set aside for 6–8 minutes. Serve scattered with grated cheese, fresh mint leaves, a sprinkle of za'atar (if using) and an extra drizzle of oil, and hand some extra grated cheese around for people to help themselves.

UNTAMED GARLIC-STUFFED POTATO SKINS

I can't help loving wild garlic (*allium ursinum*). Perhaps it is the word 'wild'. Like a rebellious adolescent, it sticks two fingers up at food corporations, shouting, 'I will grow when I want, where I want, and you cannot control me', making me laugh at the sheer joy of something that bucks all the rules.

Related to chives, with a very strong pungent aroma when rubbed between your fingers, wild garlic grows in woodlands. Be very careful not to mistake it when young for poisonous plants with similar leaves, such as lily of the valley or members of the *arum* family, as they look almost identical: the key difference is that only wild garlic has that strong smell when you rub its leaves between your fingers, but don't carry it over to another plant on your hands.

If you know where to find wild garlic growing in abundance, pick some: there is a small window in early spring when you can collect it. But as always, leave some in its natural habitat, don't strip away what's there. You can occasionally find it at farmers' markets. Grab it as soon as you see it, as it might not be there the following week.

You can make wonderful fillings for fresh pasta with it, and it makes the most delicious pesto, but I have used wild garlic in these simple stuffed jacket potato skins to make an inexpensive and quick supper. If you don't have wild garlic, you can substitute two large peeled and mashed garlic cloves, together with a small bunch of finely chopped fresh chives.

SERVES » 4

4 medium jacket potatoes

75g unsalted butter

large bunch of wild garlic, finely chopped
   (reserve some flowers and leaves
   to garnish)

150–200g grated strong cheese, such as
   mature Cheddar

sea salt and freshly ground black pepper

olive oil

a small handful of sorrel, coarsely
   chopped (optional)

Preheat the oven to 180°C/160°C fan/gas 4. Wash the potatoes and prick the skins with a fork, then bake for about 1 hour or until the centres are soft when tested with a knife point. Leave to cool, then cut in half and scoop the flesh out into a bowl, reserving the skins. Add the butter, wild garlic, cheese and seasoning to the scooped-out potato flesh and mix well.

Pile the filling up in the empty skins, then place them on a baking tray, drizzle with olive oil and bake for 25–30 minutes until golden. Serve on a large platter with the remaining wild garlic flowers and leaves as a garnish, and some chopped sorrel if you have it.

RESCUED POTATO RÖSTI WITH HERB MAYONNAISE

I spotted rösti in the supermarket freezer section recently, in a bright red packet. Rösti are so unbelievably simple and inexpensive to make that it amazed me to find there was a market for ready-made ones. So I went home and made my own to prove the point to myself. I only had old potatoes that were sprouting a little, but I knew that if I peeled them, cut out the eyes and discarded the sprouts, they would be perfectly good. The children loved them. Actually everyone loved them. They were crispy and golden on the outside and fluffy on the inside, and I felt that I'd rescued some old potatoes that had been allowed to sit for a little too long, thus avoiding food waste.

At their most simple, rösti are just made with potatoes, pre-cooked then gently grated, with salt, pepper and often a little butter added before shaping and frying. Sometimes they fall apart, so my trick is to add a little sourdough starter as I think this helps to bind the potato together and adds a superb flavour. Please note that the sourdough starter used in this recipe should be 1:1 ratio unrefreshed sourdough starter. (This means that there are equal quantities of flour and water in the starter.) The older the starter is, the more liquefied it becomes. The ratio in this recipe uses 1-week-old starter, but you may have to adjust your liquid accordingly if your starter is at a different stage or ratio. Finally, I bake these rösti in the oven, which means they're less oily.

MAKES » 6

400g potatoes, peeled and parboiled
    until almost cooked
3 tablespoons unrefreshed 1–week-old
    sourdough starter (page 192)
2 tablespoons olive oil, plus extra
    to finish
1 sprig of rosemary
salt and freshly ground black pepper
For the herb mayonnaise
3 tablespoons homemade mayonnaise
    (page 210)
a small handful of fresh herbs, such as
    parsley, chives or dill, roughly
    chopped

Preheat the oven to 180°C/160°C fan/gas 4. Roughly grate the potatoes into a bowl. Add the sourdough starter and oil, then strip the rosemary leaves from the stalk and roughly chop them, discarding the stem, and add along with the salt and black pepper. Stir until evenly mixed, then put six equal-sized dollops onto a baking tray lined with greaseproof paper and drizzle with a few more drops of olive oil.

Bake for 30 minutes until golden brown. Meanwhile, mix the mayonnaise with the roughly chopped leaves from the herbs, season well with black pepper and serve with the hot rösti.

NATURALLY GROWN MOULES MARINIÈRE

Mussels may well be the world's most sustainable meat. They are delicious, relatively inexpensive and don't damage the environment they are farmed in. The immature mussel 'spat' (a sort of larval-stage in the growth cycle), either from the wild or a specialist hatchery, attaches itself to a place to grow and simply busies itself with getting bigger, with very little human intervention.

Mussels are 'filter feeders', which means they live on microscopic plankton and other organisms containing essential nutrients, which float in the seawater around them, with no added artificial food. If mussels are raised on suspended ropes they don't come into contact with the seabed, so there is no risk of habitat destruction, although some aquaculturists grow their mussels in mesh bags or cages suspended off a pole or attached to weights.

Check that the mussels you are about to buy were not grown on the other side of the world; they live so happily in British and European waters that there's really no justification in transporting them over great distances.

A fishmonger may tell you that you can keep mussels for a few days in the fridge. I never do. I always try to buy them and use them the same day. It's just the way I was taught with anything from the sea: the fresher the better.

SERVES » 4–5

2kg mussels
75g unsalted butter
6 small shallots, finely chopped
6 garlic cloves, finely chopped
pinch of sea salt
750ml dry white wine
a large handful of chopped flat-leaf
    parsley or dill, plus extra to serve

Before using the mussels you need to lightly scrub and debeard them. Be careful not to scrub them too hard as the blue shell is delicate. If any of the mussels float as you wash them, they are not fresh, so discard them. Press the shells of any open mussels together with your finger and thumb. If they don't close, just discard them too, because a live mussel will close. Scrape off any barnacles with a sharp knife, pull out the 'beards' and drain in a colander or sieve before cooking.

Melt the butter in a large, heavy pan over a medium heat. Add the shallots, garlic and salt, and cook until soft and golden, stirring frequently. This only takes a couple of minutes.

Pour in the wine and add the parsley or dill then bring to the boil. Give the mussels a final rinse under cold water, shake and then add them to the pot. Turn them over with a large slotted spoon a couple of times, then cover and steam for about 5 minutes until the mussels open. Lift the lid halfway through cooking and give them a final stir.

They are ready to serve in the pot (remember to place a trivet or thick heatproof cloth on the table for the pan to sit on). Remove from the heat and serve with a fresh scattering of herbs, with good bread on the side (or if you like, some French fries). Don't worry about manners – dive in and use the first shell you open to pick out the mussels from all the other shells. Dip your bread, smothered in extra butter, into the cooking liquor to soak up all the flavour.

HORSE-FREE BURGERS

Few things are as good to eat as a burger on a warm summer evening. It's party food. Music playing, beer in hand, the meat sizzling on the grill. Burgers are happy food.

But the question of what goes into a 'beef' burger could really spoil the party mood. In 2013 the horsemeat scandal alerted consumers, not just in Europe but around the world, to industrial-scale meat fraud. Corrupt practices and the reduction in regulation and inspection within the international meat trade resulted in horsemeat being found in dozens of food products, from children's school dinners and supermarket lasagne to burgers in fast-food chains.

Horsemeat is similar in protein content to beef and the meat itself is not harmful, but there are many ethical issues around eating horsemeat. Many horses that end up in the food chain were originally pets or bred for racing, according to a *Guardian* investigation. As they age and pass through the hands of new owners, they can end up in the auction ring at such low prices that they become attractive to buy and process as meat.

I've been around horses all my life. Horses are sensitive, emotional and intuitive and they are easily frightened, but there is significant evidence that they are routinely subjected to brutal treatment once they pass into the meat trade and can often spend hours or even days trapped in trailers with no rest, no food and no water. There are further suggestions that horses suffer high levels of anxiety and abuse in the slaughterhouse as they panic, and unless the slaughterman has a good understanding of horse anatomy, they are not always cleanly killed.

According to recent studies, people who consume horsemeat could be at risk of being exposed to phenylbutazone, also known as bute: a non-steroid anti-inflammatory drug used regularly in domestic horses and racehorses. While this risk is, so far, theoretical, the danger to human health is not, because if it coincides with the use of paracetamol and other domestic painkillers, it can result in liver damage. But the important issue is this: you, as a consumer, should be sure of what you are buying, and on this important issue, the global food trade has let you down.

The easiest way to avoid food fraud is to buy your food from as close to the souce as possible: buy your meat direct from the farmer, use your local butcher, or look for a guarantee of local provenance in the supermarket.

SERVES » 4

For the burgers
500g minced beef
50g sourdough breadcrumbs
¼ garlic clove, crushed
3 tablespoons soy sauce
a small handful of finely chopped oregano

To serve
4 soft white baps, sliced
4 tablespoons homemade mayonnaise (page 210)
4 thin slices of cheese (optional)
1 slice of crispy smoked bacon
salad leaves and tomatoes, to dress

Put all the ingredients for the burgers in a bowl and mix well. Using your hands, shape the mixture into four equal-sized patties, squeezing each one together quite firmly. Try to make them a little wider than your baps as they will shrink slightly as they cook.

Cook under a hot grill for about 3 minutes on each side. If you like your burgers rare, then check them at this point and serve, but if you prefer them well done, cook for a further couple of minutes. Whatever you do, don't keep flipping them – homemade burgers need to be treated gently, so just cook one side before turning once to cook the other.

Spread the mayonnaise onto the bottom halves of the baps and top with the burgers, cheese (if using), bacon and a handful of salad. Cover with the tops of the baps and serve immediately.

GETTING AHEAD IN THE KITCHEN

FAIR TRADE DUQQA AND SOURDOUGH FLATBREADS

This is a recipe made for sharing, with aromatic spices, the texture of toasted hazelnuts, warm flatbreads and green grassy olive oil. It is the kind of food that you put down in the middle of the table when you want to chat with friends about life.

Ten years ago it was almost impossible to buy fair trade spices, now they are much easier to find. A fair trade logo tells you that farmers and workers in developing countries are within a scheme that aims to get them a fair price for their crop, and helps improve education and environmental standards within the farming community.

Duqqa will stay fragrant for up to a week in an airtight container, so you can make it ahead. The flatbreads will keep for three days wrapped in a cotton tea towel – simply warm before serving.

MAKES » 6

For the duqqa
200g blanched hazelnuts
2 tablespoons sesame seeds
1 tablespoon coriander seeds
1 tablespoon cumin seeds
½ tablespoon fennel seeds
¼ teaspoon whole black peppercorns
1 teaspoon sea salt
a good handful of fresh mint, very finely
    chopped, and some olive oil, to serve
For the sourdough flatbreads
250g warm water (at 28°C)
100g levain (page 196)
220g wholemeal flour (my favourite
    is Khorasan)
220g strong white bread flour, plus
    extra for dusting
1 teaspoon sea salt,
    plus extra to garnish
3 tablespoons cumin seeds, toasted in
    a frying pan
For the eggwash
20ml water
20g plain yogurt (page 199)
1 egg, beaten
½ teaspoon fine sea salt

To make the duqqa, warm a heavy-based frying pan over a medium heat, add the hazelnuts and toast them gently, stirring occasionally for 4–5 minutes until golden, then tip them onto a plate and leave to cool. Next, add the sesame, coriander, cumin and fennel seeds along with the peppercorns to the pan. Toast, stirring continuously, for about 1–2 minutes until fragrant, then remove from the heat and leave to cool. Put the nuts and spices into a pestle and mortar, add the salt and coarsely grind the mixture (you can use a food processor, but don't over-process the mixture).

To make the sourdough flatbreads, mix the water and levain together in a bowl. Stir in the flours, salt, and cumin seeds, and leave for 10 minutes. Then knead the dough for about 4 minutes on a lightly floured worktop, cover the bowl and transfer to the fridge overnight; or leave on the side in the kitchen until it has roughly doubled in size.

Preheat the oven to 220°C/200°C fan/gas 7 and if you have one, put a baking stone inside: I use a metal Welsh bakestone that is excellent at holding the heat. Otherwise, have a couple of baking trays ready.

Scrape the dough onto a lightly floured work surface, flour the top and pat it out flattish, then divide it into six equal pieces. One at a time, work each piece of dough out with your hands to a circle about 15–20cm in diameter (depending on how thick you want your flatbreads) by pressing down firmly onto the dough with your fingertips and stretching it gently. Turn the bread 90 degrees and repeat to make a dimpled grid pattern in the dough with your fingertips.

Mix all the eggwash ingredients together in a bowl and lightly brush the top of each piece of dough with it. Place the dough on trays in the oven or use a bakers' peel to slide the pieces one at a time onto the baking stone, and bake for 12–15 minutes until golden.

Once baked, transfer the flatbreads to a wire rack and serve while still warm (or reheat the breads in a hot oven for a couple of minutes before serving). Serve with the duqqa, mint and a bowl of olive oil. (You can mix the mint into the duqqa to serve, if you like.)

SEASONAL HOMEMADE PESTO

Now here's a thing – it's not just basil that you can turn into pesto. The name is derived from the Genoese dialect word, *pestâ*, which simply means '*to pound*', because it was made using a mortar and pestle, so it's about the method and texture rather than a particular ingredient.

By using whatever herbs are in season, you can make this fresh, vibrant and versatile paste almost all year round, particularly if you can keep a few things growing in pots on a sunny windowsill, to extend the normal growing season you'd have in your garden.

A single packet of seeds costs less than the price of a packet of herbs flown in from thousands of miles away, so once you have established some pots of herbs you can make this pesto for next to nothing. Plant soft-leaf herbs like oregano, tarragon, parsley, basil, coriander or dill, and early in the season the first shoots will appear. You can keep on picking them throughout the summer and autumn, and well into winter in the case of parsley.

If you think you don't have space for herbs, then look again for somewhere you can grow them. You'd be surprised what a wonderful thing sharing is. Talk to your neighbours and ask if they would be interested in sharing some space for herbs, or your parish council might need local window- or planting-boxes tended. Sometimes, independently owned pubs are delighted to have some herbs growing in the pub garden, or find a local community garden. Get out there. Look for opportunities and then, boom: you meet people, you laugh, you chat and you share. This is the life. Then make a huge pan of pasta and invite everyone round. I promise it feels great.

MAKES » 1x350ml JAR

1 small garlic clove
150g nuts, such as pine nuts, hazelnuts,
   brazil nuts, but if you can find
   local cobnuts even better
a large handful of grated hard cheese
a handful of fresh garden herbs
150ml olive oil, plus extra to cover
sea salt and freshly ground black pepper

Using a pestle and mortar rather than a blender, smash up the garlic, add the nuts and blend. Add the cheese and chop the herbs into 2mm lengths using scissors. Mix in, then add the olive oil just a few drops at a time, mixing until you get the consistency you like. I find I use almost an equal measure to the nuts. Season with salt and black pepper. Your pesto is ready to use. To store, spoon into clean, sterilised jars and cover with a 5mm layer of olive oil. It will keep for 3–4 days in the fridge.

GETTING THE MOST FROM JUNIPER-
AND GIN-CURED SALMON

One of the great things about curing a side of salmon yourself is that there is very little waste. Freezing it first kills any lurking parasites (*see below*). The curing essentially 'cooks' it, and you can then use any leftovers in pasta dishes, in fishcakes, or in any way that you'd use smoked salmon.

You do have to be choosy when you're shopping for fresh salmon. There are not plenty more fish in the sea. On the one hand, the Marine Stewardship Council (MSC) says that Atlantic wild-caught salmon stocks are severely depleted; and on the other, we know that poorly managed salmon farms can spread diseases and parasites, that some overuse chemicals and that fish-waste disposal can seriously affect marine ecosystems.

So the best way to shop for salmon is to choose fish from undepleted stocks: either MSC-certified sustainable Pacific salmon from Alaska or organically farmed Atlantic salmon, where practices don't fall foul of the guidelines. That way you can at least be assured that you're buying the most sustainable fish out there.

SERVES » 6

1 tablespoon coriander seeds
2 tablespoons juniper berries, plus
    1 tablespoon extra
zest of 3 oranges
zest of 1 lime
zest of 1 grapefruit
40ml gin
250g sea salt
375g soft brown sugar
1 side fillet of very fresh salmon, weighing
    about 750g, skin removed and frozen
    first (see right)
large sprig of rosemary
5 star anise
a handful of fresh dill, to garnish
horseradish sauce, beetroot salad and
    rye toast, to serve

You can either put the seeds, berries, zests, gin, salt and sugar into a blender and whizz them together, or use a large pestle and mortar to grind first the coriander seeds, then the juniper berries, mixing both with the sugar and salt and grinding again, and then adding and 'bruising' the zests and finally stirring in the gin.

Place the salmon in a long ovenproof dish and cover it in the gin mixture (it must be submerged, so increase the quantity of the marinade if necessary). Scatter over the rosemary, star anise and extra juniper berries, then cover the dish with a lid and leave it in the fridge for 24 hours.

To serve, lift the fish out of the marinade, wipe off any bits and lay it on a serving platter before finely slicing it. Snip the dill into small sprigs and scatter over the top. Serve with fresh horseradish sauce, a beetroot salad and rye toast with lime wedges and a stiff gin and tonic.

Freezing the salmon

All wild fish and some farmed fish are known to be at risk of harbouring parasites, including tapeworms, flukes and a roundworm called anisakis. The risk is less in western Europe, and these critters are all destroyed by thorough cooking to at least 60°C. But if you plan to eat fish raw, lightly cooked or cured, then it should be frozen at -15°C or lower, for at least four days before thawing and using (some sources suggest -20°C for seven days). All fish purchased from reputable sources will have been frozen, but if you catch the fish yourself, make sure that your domestic freezer is capable of the required level of coldness.

BEAN OVERLOOKED FUL MEDAMES

This delicious spicy stew that's traditionally eaten for breakfast may be the national dish of Egypt and available throughout North Africa and the Levant, but just because you are cooking a recipe from the other side of the Mediterranean doesn't mean that your ingredients need travel long distances too.

The main ingredient is dried broad beans, known in French as 'fèves', or more commonly, fava beans. What surprised me was finding out that not only are broad beans thought to be one of the oldest cultivated crops grown in Britain, but that they are still quite widely grown in Norfolk, often for export to the Middle East. Broad beans are also a great crop for sustainable agriculture: as a legume, they help to fix nitrogen in the soil for whatever is grown in the field the following year, and their scented flowers are attractive to bees and other pollinating insects. Add to that the fact that they are hardy and easy to grow, and that they are high in protein and rich in vitamin C, and I wonder why we fail to make more of this reliable, traditional crop. Try growing some in a sunny, sheltered corner of your own garden.

SERVES » 8–12

1kg whole dried broad beans
2 onions, finely chopped
3 heaped teaspoons cumin seeds
100ml olive oil, plus extra to serve
2 garlic cloves, finely chopped
juice of 2–3 large lemons
¾ teaspoon chilli powder
½ teaspoon cayenne pepper
¼ teaspoon ground cinnamon
750ml passata
3 tablespoons tomato purée
a handful of chopped fresh herbs,
    such as coriander or parsley
2–3 heaped teaspoons granulated sugar
sea salt and freshly ground black pepper
150g feta-style cheese, crumbled
2–3 red or green chillies, finely chopped
2–3 tablespoons toasted chopped
    pistachios

Tip the dried beans into a large pan, cover with cold water and leave to soak overnight. The following day, drain the beans, return to the pan, cover with cold water and bring to the boil. Reduce the heat and simmer for about 1 hour until tender, stirring occasionally. When the beans are soft, drain thoroughly.

In a separate large pan, sauté the onions and cumin seeds gently in a little of the olive oil until lightly cooked. Then add the remaining oil with the garlic, lemon juice, chilli, cayenne and cinnamon.

Stir in the passata and tomato purée. Cook for another minute or so, then add the drained beans. Add the herbs, reserving some to garnish, and simmer for a further 20 minutes. Add the sugar and season with salt and black pepper. You can reduce the sauce further if you prefer it thicker.

To serve, scatter with the crumbled cheese, chopped chillies and pistachios. Garnish with the remaining chopped herbs, a few twists of black pepper and a good drizzle of olive oil.

FEWER FOOD MILES FARMERS' MARKET MINESTRONE SOUP

To say I love going to a farmers' market to buy our food is an understatement. I *really* love it. I love the banter, the sense of community, the sights and smells, and the fresh produce. I really believe that connecting with the farmers makes my food taste better. I can't promise though that shopping here is cheaper because this is not mass-produced food; it is from small producers, grown locally and in season. The invisible benefit is that because what's on sale hasn't been airfreighted around the world before you can buy it, you're cutting down on food miles, which means you're doing something to reduce carbon dioxide emissions.

There is also huge value in chatting directly with the farmer and building a relationship, as this gives you a unique understanding of your food: reminding you that you are investing your money in your local economy. It feels right.

I think that minestrone soup can be the perfect farmers' market meal, if you excuse the presence of one or two Italian ingredients. You can easily leave out the bacon and cheese if you prefer a vegan version, and do use substitutes for any vegetables that are out of season.

SERVES » 6

3–4 rashers of thick-cut smoked bacon
20g unsalted butter
3 tablespoons rapeseed oil
2 large red onions
3 large carrots
1 medium potato
7 sprigs of lemon thyme
2 bay leaves
100g green beans
1.5 litres hot vegetable stock
a couple of 5cm pieces of Parmesan
    rind (optional)
6 large tomatoes
2 x 250g cans cannellini beans
1 small cabbage, shredded
a handful of fresh green herbs, such as
    parsley, basil or oregano
grated Parmesan, to serve

Chop the bacon into 1.5cm squares and fry with the butter and oil over a low heat. Meanwhile, peel and slice the onions then add them to the sizzling bacon. Reduce the heat to really low; keep stirring every now and again until the onions are soft but still translucent. Peel and dice the carrots and potato, then strip the thyme leaves and discard the stems. Add the chopped vegetables, thyme and bay leaves to the pan.

Keep the heat on low and stir for a further 5 minutes. Chop the green beans into 1.5cm lengths and add these with the vegetable stock and Parmesan rinds, if using. Cut an 'X' into the bottom of each tomato and add them to the pan whole.

Bring the soup to the boil then reduce the heat to a simmer. Cover with a lid set slightly askew and leave it to simmer for 1½ hours, giving it an occasional stir to stop anything catching on the bottom of the pan.

Once the soup has cooked, remove and discard the tomato skins, bay leaves and Parmesan rinds. Drain the cannellini beans, rinse them under cold running water, then add them to the soup along with the cabbage. Cook for a further 10 minutes. Finally, stir in the herbs and serve piping hot with grated Parmesan.

POLE-AND-LINE-CAUGHT TUNA FISHCAKES with minted peas

Homemade fishcakes are a classic, and this is a recipe I return to time and time again for a quick, inexpensive supper, as the fishcakes can be made in advance and cooked straight from the freezer. They also make a great substitute for burgers. However, picking the 'right' tuna to use is not as straightforward as you might imagine.

The environmental activist organisation Client Earth published a survey in 2011 showing that 32 out of 100 fish products examined made misleading or unverified claims such as 'protects the marine environment'. Many 'dolphin-friendly' labels on canned tuna simply referred to catches where dolphins were not at risk, such as skipjack tuna (the one tuna species that dolphins don't associate with) but failed to report on either the sustainability of the tuna population or the extent to which other species such as turtles, sharks, marlin and dorado were being caught and needlessly killed in the hunt for tuna. What is immediately clear is that for the tuna we buy to be truly sustainable, the only fishing method is the pole-and-line method because the only thing that catches is tuna. The words 'dolphin friendly' are not necessarily enough.

MAKES »8

For the fishcakes

4 tablespoons rapeseed oil

1 spring onion, finely chopped

2 garlic cloves, finely chopped

2.5cm piece of fresh root ginger, peeled and finely chopped or crushed

1 teaspoon five spice powder

3 x 150g cans tuna in spring water, drained

350g mashed potato

3 tablespoons dark soy sauce

a handful of freshly chopped basil

grated zest and juice of 2 limes

sea salt and freshly ground black pepper

1 medium egg, beaten

100g breadcrumbs, either fresh or dry

4 tablespoon sesame seed oil

For the crushed minted peas

600g fresh shelled peas, or thawed frozen ones

75g unsalted butter

a handful of finely chopped fresh mint

zest and juice of 1 lemon

salt and freshly ground black pepper

Heat a large saucepan, add half the rapeseed oil and lightly sauté the spring onion. Add the garlic and ginger and cook for about 30 seconds. Add the five spice, stir well, then add the tuna and mashed potato. Mix well over a low heat.

Add the soy sauce and basil then add the lime zest and juice, and season with salt and black pepper. Remove from the heat and leave to cool for a few minutes.

Shape the mixture into eight fishcakes, coat well in the beaten egg and then the breadcrumbs: you can freeze them at this point. Mix together the remaining rapeseed oil with the sesame oil then pour half of this into a very large frying pan. Fry the fishcakes over a medium heat until golden brown. Cook on one side, add the rest of the oil, then carefully flip the fishcakes to cook the other side. Don't keep flipping them over, as this can make them break up. Keep these warm until you're ready to serve.

To make the minted peas, pulse the peas twice in a food processer to break them down but do not completely purée them. Remove one third of the pulsed peas and continue to purée the remaining two thirds.

Transfer both the coarse and puréed peas to a large, heavy-based saucepan and add the butter and mint. Cook the pea mixture over a low heat with the lid on for 5 minutes. Stir in the lemon zest, cook for a further 3 minutes then stir in the lemon juice and season to taste. Serve hot with the fishcakes.

LOCAL HERO LEEK, FETA AND NASTURTIUM QUICHE

I love capers. Like anchovies, they add an intensity, especially to things like quiches, fish and asparagus, and they work amazingly well with lemon. But even though they are small and light, and the weight/food miles equation is hardly devastating, part of being a food activist is questioning how much of our food really needs importing and then exploring the alternatives. So sometimes I just use other ingredients at hand: perhaps crisp fried onions, chillies or garlic slivers. At other times, I just add more fresh herbs to amplify the flavour. But occasionally, I find almost forgotten locally sourced ingredients that work just as well. This quiche uses a nasturtium seed pods that I pickled from my garden, which taste very much like capers – an old ingredient that we could use more often, but that sounds more like a crazy new idea.

One of the reasons I love this recipe is that you can make the pastry up to two days in advance, and sauté the leeks and mix the eggs and milk the day before baking. Keep them all in the fridge and it's a simple 'assemble and cook' exercise when you are ready.

SERVES » 4-6

For the pastry

225g plain white flour, plus extra
    for dusting
100g unsalted butter, diced
pinch of salt

For the filling

1 medium leek, washed and
    finely chopped
20g unsalted butter
10g sunflower oil
2 sprigs of lemon thyme, leaves only
150g feta-style cheese
2 tablespoons pickled nasturtium seed
    pods (see right)
40g grated Parmesan-style cheese
140ml whole milk or cream
3 large eggs

For the pickled nasturtiums

60g sea salt
150g fresh green nasturtium seed pods
approx. 350ml cider vinegar
1 teaspoon black peppercorns
3 small fresh red chillies
1 clove
2 bay leaves

Preheat the oven to 220°C/200°C fan/gas 7. Put all the pastry ingredients into a bowl. Using the tips of your fingers work the butter into the flour until it resembles breadcrumbs. Add 2 tablespoons of cold water and bring the dough together into a ball. Do not overwork the dough as it will activate the gluten in the flour and make it tough.

Roll the dough out onto a lightly floured work surface to about 0.5cm thick and use this to line a greased or non-stick ovenproof 25cm quiche dish or deep tart tin. Cover the pastry with non-stick baking paper, fill with ceramic beads, then blind bake in the lower third of the oven for 10 minutes. Remove from the oven and leave to cool. Turn the oven off.

Meanwhile, make the filling by sautéing the leek with the butter, oil and lemon thyme leaves until soft. Leave to cool. When you are ready to bake, preheat the oven to 180°C/160°C fan/gas 4 and spoon the leeks into the pastry case with the feta, nasturtium seeds and Parmesan, reserving a little feta and Parmesan for the top. Whisk together the milk or cream and eggs in a bowl then pour into the case. Top with the reserved cheese and bake for 25–30 minutes until the filling is puffy and golden.

PICKLED NASTURTIUMS

Nasturtium plants are beautiful, and the leaves and flowers make fantastic additions to salads during the summer, as long as you haven't sprayed them with any chemicals as they were growing. They grow best in dry soil, and the seed pods are best picked while still unripe and green. I don't collect a huge quantity of them, but a cupful from about a dozen plants is enough for pickling to use in place of capers, and there is a huge amount of both flavour and satisfaction in using anything you've grown.

Mix the sea salt with enough cold water to cover the seed pods by about 2.5cm in a clean jam jar (use about 350ml of water), and put the pods in the jar with the brine. Leave for 24 hours. Drain the seed pods and rinse well.

Put the amount of cider vinegar that would fill the jar into a small saucepan, add the peppercorns, chillies, clove and bay leaves and bring to the boil. Boil for about 2 minutes.

Repack the seeds into a sterilised jar and cover with the boiling spiced vinegar, making sure the bay leaves and all the spices go into the jar, and seal. Set aside for 21 days to mature before using.

FIRM FRIENDS PASTIES

Show me a man who doesn't love a pasty. In fact, show me anyone who doesn't love one. A warm, golden-crusted potato pasty oozing melted cheese is irresistible. But when you buy a 'genuine' Cornish pasty from a major manufacturer and find palm oil or hydrogenated fat in the pastry, it's so disappointing... I'd rather make my own.

Except that I can't make pasties alone. Well, I can, but I'd be missing out on the fun. Sometimes, caring about what we eat is better with friends, so I have pasty-making parties. Honestly, I do. Get together with two or three friends, put on some fun music, relax with a glass of wine and have a good time. And everyone goes home with a batch of pasties for the freezer.

This recipe gives quantities for each person to make six pasties, so simply multiply the amounts by the number of people who'll be partying together, or give each guest their personal shopping list. You can vary the fillings according to what you have on hand; here, I've used bacon and toasted cumin seeds for extra flavour, but you could stir a tablespoon of redcurrant jelly into the potatoes and use a Brie-style local cheese instead of Cheddar. Or try goat's cheese and chive, or Stilton and some chunky cooked mushrooms; even a drained can of tuna, with sweetcorn. It really is up to you to add what you want to the potato – as long as the mixture is firm enough to fill the pasty, it's good to use.

SERVES » 6

1 tablespoon cumin seeds

3 tablespoons rapeseed or olive oil

2 onions, cut into rings

3–4 spring onions, chopped

400g potatoes, peeled, cut into small, even-sized chunks and boiled

275g Cheddar cheese, cut into 1cm cubes

8–10 rashers of cooked bacon, chopped

a handful of chopped fresh herbs, such as chives, oregano, dill or parsley

salt and freshly ground black pepper

double quantity of Fair and Simple Shortcrust Pastry (page 206)

1 medium egg, beaten with 1–2 tablespoons milk

Toast the cumin seeds for 1 minute in a large, dry, heavy saucepan until fragrant. Tip onto a plate and set aside, then add the oil to the pan and put over a medium heat. Once the oil is hot, add the onions and fry until golden. Add the spring onions and toasted cumin seeds then add the cooked potatoes. Mash roughly then leave to cool. Stir in the cheese, bacon and herbs. Mix well and season with salt and black pepper and leave the mixture to cool.

Divide the pastry into six equal pieces, rolling each one out onto a lightly floured surface into circles about 18cm in diameter, or slightly larger, and 5mm thick. Pile the filling onto one half of each piece, following the curve of the pastry but leaving a 1.5cm clear border around the edge. Brush this with the beaten egg, then fold the half with no filling over the top of the potato mixture and press it down firmly to seal in a half-moon shape. Transfer to a baking tray lined with non-stick paper and brush the tops with the remaining eggwash. Using a sharp knife, make 1.5cm slashes in the tops to allow any steam to escape, then either bake in an oven at 180°C/160°C fan/gas 4 for 20 minutes, or place in the freezer (stored in a ziplock bag). They take just 5 minutes longer to bake from frozen.

NO KIDDING SHEPHERD'S PIE

My favourite cheese is goat's cheese, which is not surprising because when most of my friends had a pet gerbil, I had a pet goat called Penny, and one of my jobs was to milk her. Then I'd take the pail into the kitchen where my mum would add lemon juice to make curds and whey, which were strained to make cheese. I have vivid memories of Penny standing on her hind legs, leaning into the kitchen while I fed her slices of bread. Kids (the goat sort) are playful, full of character, inquisitive and oh so mischievous.

There is, though, a hidden cost to goat's cheese. Defra estimates that about 200,000 kids are born in the UK each year, but almost all the males are killed at birth, because they are not seen as valuable (they don't grow up to give milk).

With a little help from us, that can change. There's now a venture taking young billies from dairy goat farms so they can be reared for their meat, to high welfare standards. Yes, the end result is still the death of the animal, because that is the result of livestock farming; but to euthanase them at birth seems to me more wasteful of their lives. It takes no more resources to raise a male kid than a female, and if one can give us milk, surely the other can also feed us. There's then a secondary problem, because the UK doesn't really have a tradition of eating goat meat, unlike parts of the Caribbean, Latin America, Africa and South Asia. Even in southern Italy and Greece, you'll often find roast goat served at Easter, but the British so far have not been converted. So this venture is also working hard to get goat meat onto restaurant menus, seeing this as a quicker way to secure a foothold in the market than by trying to sell to the average domestic consumer. But I think that if we can make goat something we all occasionally purchase, we can do so much more to address the current ethical problem we've failed to recognise behind the goat's milk and cheeses available in our supermarkets.

I can't promise that this is a cheap recipe to make, but you can substitute Puy lentils for half the meat to reduce the cost.

SERVES » 4–6

1.25kg potatoes, peeled and diced

175g unsalted butter, diced small

salt and freshly ground black pepper

2 tablespoons coconut oil

3 medium onions, diced

2 medium carrots, peeled and diced

3 sticks of celery, chopped

750g goat meat, minced

3 bay leaves

1 sprig of lemon thyme

1 teaspoon ras el hanout

400ml hot lamb stock

2 tablespoons cornflour

Boil the potatoes in salted water until soft, drain and mash in the pan with 150g of the butter. Season with salt and black pepper and set aside.

Add the coconut oil to a separate large saucepan over a medium heat, then add the vegetables and sauté until softened. Add the goat meat, about one third at a time, and cook until browned before adding the next batch. Stir in the herbs and spices then pour in the stock. Simmer for 1 hour, stirring regularly. Do check for dryness and add a little water if necessary.

Mix the cornflour with 5–6 tablespoons of cold water to form a smooth paste. Whisk this into the sauce to thicken. Transfer to an ovenproof dish and top with the mashed potato. Run a fork over the top to fluff up the mash and scatter with the remaining butter.

You can keep the pie in the fridge for up to 48 hours. When you are ready to cook, preheat the oven to 180°C/160°C fan/gas 4 and bake for 35–40 minutes until the mash is golden and the filling piping hot.

BIODIVERSITY CHOCOLATE CHIP COOKIES

Some years ago when a large agricultural group attempted large-scale, intensive production of cocoa, it failed. They cleared the rainforest, planted trees in neat rows, used chemical fertilisers, herbicides and pesticides and aggressively removed other plants and wildlife from the rainforest floor to make way for high-yielding cocoa. It was designed to give the biggest return possible in the shortest time, but the cocoa pods did not appear. The trees failed to produce fruit and, as it turned out, it was because the insects had nowhere to live or breed and so the flowers did not get pollinated.

Nature doesn't always play ball. Apart from the fact that continuous monoculture, where the same crop is grown on a piece of land year after year, can speed up the development of specialised pests and diseases, and then spread them rapidly across the entire area, there's a more practical problem. Most of the world's flowers are pollinated by species of bees, hoverflies, butterflies and moths, or even beetles. However, cocoa can only be pollinated by a midge: a tiny fly, which is uniquely able to negotiate the shape of the cocoa flower; and the flowers die within 24 hours if not pollinated when they open. But this insect is not at home on the clean, single-plant estate. It needs humid shade and what we might think of as 'natural' tropical conditions: a variety of plant species growing in harmony and decaying matter on the ground.

So the bigger a cocoa plantation gets, the less likely it is that the midges will find their way round the lines of cleanly planted trees; bringing us closer to the potential future chocolate shortage that the large manufacturers sometimes make grumbling noises about. My reason for telling you this is simply to underline something: that encouraging you to buy chocolate made from cocoa beans grown on small farms which use the most sustainable practices actually helps to protect biodiversity, because the farmers don't just grow their trees in sterile, cocoa-only rows. Smaller and wilder plantings are good for nature, good for the cocoa trees themselves, better for the farmers (where they are protected by fair trade agreements) and help to secure the supply of cocoa over the long term. So you have every reason to look for fair trade and sustainable cocoa powder and dark chocolate when you come to bake.

Rich, soft and sweet, these unbelievably good cookies are a doddle to make. You can freeze them, unbaked, once they're on the tray and then keep them in the freezer in a ziplock bag for up to three months. There have been many times when I have whipped these out of the freezer to look like a total domestic goddess with a tray of immaculate biscuits, ready in a matter of minutes.

MAKES » 24

225g self-raising flour
pinch of sea salt
225g soft brown sugar
50g cocoa powder
125g unsalted butter, softened, plus
    extra for greasing
1 large egg
75g nuts of your choice or cherries,
    chopped
150g dark chocolate (70 per cent cocoa
    solids), chopped into small pieces

Sift the flour, salt, sugar and cocoa powder into a large bowl and mix well. Add the butter and egg and mix until a ball of dough is formed. Add the nuts or cherries along with the chocolate and mix for a further 1–2 minutes until evenly distributed.

Preheat the oven to 180°C/160°C fan/gas 4.

Roll the dough into walnut-sized balls with your hands and place them onto a lightly greased baking tray. Bake for 10–12 minutes. The cookies will still be soft after 12 minutes, but resist the temptation to bake them until they are hard, as they will then be crunchy instead of soft. Remove the tray from the oven and leave the cookies for a few minutes to allow the chocolate to set a little before transferring them to a wire rack to cool.

LONG, LEISURELY WEEKEND FOOD

FEET-IN-THE-SOIL ORANGE, LEMON AND DILL BUTTERNUT SQUASH LASAGNE

Chefs will tell you that good food starts with good ingredients. But the truth is, it starts before the food is even grown: with good soil. Our ingredients come from the earth, yet it's a connection that all too often we forget: the soil makes the food. As a gardener I am reminded of the relationship we have with our planet when I sow seeds or plant cuttings. Healthy soil means healthy plants. And in turn, healthy plants make healthy people.

The butternut squash, wheat, herbs and spinach in this recipe came straight from the ground, organically grown and sustainably cultivated; the coconut, nutmeg, oranges and lemons from trees, which in turn had their roots in the soil. This is the earth that sustains us. The task we all have is to work towards the earth being healthy, not polluted with chemicals or plastic waste; because the health of our planet will in the end determine our future.

This sunny Caribbean-flavoured vegetarian recipe is such a cheery dish. Layers of orange butternut squash, bright green spinach and creamy nutmeg-infused coconut sauce, all topped with crunchy sourdough breadcrumbs.

SERVES » 6

For the butternut squash

3 tablespoons coconut oil

1kg peeled butternut squash,
    cut into 4cm cubes

4 sprigs of rosemary, leaves only,
    finely chopped

finely grated zest of 2 large unwaxed
    lemons

1 teaspoon sea salt

For the coconut sauce

50g coconut oil

50g plain flour

400ml can coconut milk

1 teaspoon freshly grated nutmeg

sea salt and freshly ground black pepper

To assemble the lasagne

9 large lasagne sheets

sea salt and olive oil

100g spinach leaves, roughly chopped

a large handful of fresh parsley, chopped

500g ricotta cheese, crumbled

freshly ground black pepper

For the breadcrumb topping

75g strong hard cheese, such as
    Parmesan

75g sourdough breadcrumbs

2 garlic cloves, peeled and finely
    chopped

finely grated zest of 1 orange

a handful of fresh dill, chopped

Preheat the oven to 180°C/160°C fan/gas 4. Put the coconut oil in a large shallow roasting tray in the oven for 1 minute to warm. Then add the butternut squash, rosemary, lemon zest and salt. Toss the squash in the oil and roast for 30–40 minutes or until it is very tender when poked with a fork. Remove from the oven (switch the oven off), mash, and set aside.

Next, make the coconut sauce. Mix together the coconut oil and flour in a saucepan. Cook over a medium heat for 2 minutes, stirring often. Add the coconut milk a little at a time, mixing until you have a smooth sauce. Stir in the nutmeg with salt and black pepper to taste, then set aside.

Cook the lasagne sheets for 5 minutes in a large pan of salted boiling water with a tablespoon of olive oil until the sheets have softened. Drain the sheets and drizzle with olive oil so they don't stick together while cooling.

Preheat the oven to 180°C/160°C fan/gas 4. Finally, assemble the lasagne. Layer about one third of the butternut squash into a deep 20cm x 27cm dish, followed by one third of the spinach leaves, one third of the ricotta and a good grind of black pepper, then 3 lasagne sheets followed by a thin layer of coconut sauce. Repeat this layering twice more. To finish, spoon over the remaining coconut sauce. Mix the breadcrumb topping ingredients together in a bowl and spread the mixture in an even layer over the top of the white sauce. Bake for 30–40 minutes or until piping hot and golden.

EASY CONSCIENCE SEASONAL VEGETABLE CURRY

As a student I lived in Leicester for three years at the back of an Indian restaurant. Curry is still my idea of heaven; warm spices are so often the antidote to British weather!

After a few years of hanging out with my mates enjoying regular fiery and fragrant feasts, I noticed that there was an automatic assumption that curry had to involve some kind of meat. The choice was chicken, mutton or lamb (more often than not), occasionally beef and sometimes goat. The provenance of the meat was never mentioned, and eventually, I started to wonder about that, and about who had grown and harvested the spices that were in the curry. My mind would wander as I laughed and chatted with my gang, wondering whether the people who grew our spices also had their friends and families round for the evening, and if they had the luxury of a cold beer and a chance to catch up.

So this is about having an easy conscience – by making the most ethical curry in the world with a recipe to celebrate. It relies upon you choosing to buy and cook with fair trade spices, organic coconut oil, seasonal vegetables and local honey and yogurt, with herbs grown in your garden or in a pot on the windowsill. But make sure you save on food miles by choosing veggies that are local and in season; you might substitute butternut squash, fresh spinach leaves, tomatoes, mangetout or sugar snap peas (or a big handful of podded peas), whole green beans, discs of carrot or even mushrooms for what's in the recipe, cut into different shapes, to give the dish visual appeal.

SERVES » 4–6

2 large potatoes, unpeeled

6 tablespoons coconut oil

1 stick of cinnamon

2 star anise

2 tablespoons mustard seeds

2 tablespoons cumin seeds

2 tablespoons fennel seeds

2 large onions, chopped

2 tablespoons garam masala

2 tablespoons mild curry powder

1 tablespoon sea salt

seasonal local vegetables, such as

    2 courgettes, cut into 1cm thick slices

    1 aubergine, cut into sticks the size of your little finger

    ½ cauliflower, broken into florets

2 tablespoons coconut yogurt

For the yogurt dressing

200g plain yogurt

1 teaspoon turmeric

1 tablespoon honey

½ teaspoon sea salt

4 sprigs of mint, roughly chopped (optional)

a handful of coriander or parsley leaves

Cook the potatoes whole for 10 minutes then drain, and chop into 2.5cm cubes, leaving the skin on. Put the coconut oil, cinnamon and star anise in a saucepan and heat. Add the mustard, cumin and fennel seeds and onions, and sauté until the onions are soft and caramelised. It will be very fragrant as you cook.

Once the onions are soft and dark, add the garam masala, curry powder and salt, then stir in the seasonal vegetables and diced potatoes. Stir well and cook for a further 5–6 minutes until the vegetables are well coated with spices and just starting to soften. Add a little more coconut oil if necessary. Reduce the heat, add about 120ml cold water and cook for a further 5 minutes until the vegetables are soft but still have some shape. Remove from the heat, cover with a lid and leave for 15 minutes, then stir in the coconut yogurt.

Meanwhile, make the yogurt dressing. Stir the yogurt, turmeric, honey, salt and mint (if using) together in a small bowl. Spoon the curry into a serving dish and scatter coriander or parsley leaves over the top. Serve with the yogurt dressing on the side

Great with a big bowl of steamed or boiled basmati rice to share.

HALVE THE MEAT MOUSSAKA

When my conscience pricks me, I think that the only ethical way to eat is vegan, but every time I suggest this in our house, it falls flat. I've got some committed carnivores in my family, and if I ask them to give up meat completely, they just refuse, holding on to their craving for cooked animal flesh like a dog holding on to its favourite bone.

I don't think I'd miss meat, but many people aren't ready to give it up, despite genuinely caring about the environment. It doesn't have to be an all-or-nothing decision. This recipe is a halfway point, a delicious compromise: a meal that is both as comfortable as an old friend and a little kinder to the planet. Using organic local lamb but halving the amount of meat, means I can still support local farmers and reduce my food miles, while putting a little less pressure on clean water, farmland and chemical fertilisers. And you can take it from me – even hardcore carnivores will love the end result.

SERVES » 6

1 tablespoon cumin seeds
4 tablespoons olive oil
2 medium onions, finely chopped
3 garlic cloves, finely chopped
2 level teaspoons ground cinnamon
350g minced lamb
400g can Puy lentils, drained
    (approx. 240g)
200ml red or white wine
400g can chopped tomatoes
1 teaspoon sugar
salt and freshly ground black pepper
2 handfuls of fresh oregano, chopped
3 medium aubergines, sliced into
    5mm rounds
500g potatoes, peeled
For the béchamel sauce
600ml whole milk
2–3 bay leaves
75g butter
75g plain flour
100g strong cheese, grated
2 medium eggs, beaten
salt and freshly ground black pepper
½ teaspoon freshly grated nutmeg

Dry roast the cumin seeds for 2 minutes in a pan and set aside. Then in the same pan, using a little of the oil, sauté the onions until soft. Add the garlic, cinnamon and lamb and continue frying until the meat is browned and fully cooked. Stir in the cumin seeds, lentils and wine and cook over a high heat for 5–6 minutes. Add the tomatoes and simmer over a very low heat for 45 minutes–1 hour. Stir in the sugar, season with salt and black pepper and half the oregano. Remove from the heat, cool, then set aside for a few hours, or preferably in the fridge overnight.

Preheat the oven to 180°C/160°C fan/gas 4. Oil some baking trays, layer the aubergines on them and brush with more oil. Bake for about 30 minutes or until soft. Meanwhile, cook the potatoes in boiling water for 5 minutes then drain in a colander under running water until cold. Slice thinly.

To make the béchamel sauce, warm the milk and bay leaves and leave to infuse, preferably overnight. The following day, melt the butter in a large saucepan and bring the milk to just below boiling point. Stir the flour into the butter and cook for 2 minutes, then add the hot milk a little at a time over a low heat, stirring constantly with a wooden spoon. Cook until you have a thick sauce then stir in the cheese. Remove from the heat and leave to cool for a couple of minutes, then whisk in the eggs, season with salt and black peppper and add the nutmeg.

Lay one third of the aubergines in the base of a large dish, cover with half the meat then half the potatoes. Repeat, and finish with a final layer of aubergines. Top with the sauce. Bake for about 45 minutes until golden, scatter the rest of the oregano on top, leave to cool for 3 minutes and serve.

WITH INTEGRITY HOMEMADE BAKED BEANS

The humble baked bean might seem one of the most ethical foods you can buy. Vegan, high fibre, gluten free (if you can manage without toast!), available in low-sugar and low-salt varieties, with no artificial flavourings, preservatives, or sweeteners like fructose syrup. I'm very particular about how I eat my beans: on white, tight-crumbed sourdough toast, cut medium–thick and left to go crunchy in the toaster, then slathered with cold salted butter; and the beans have to be HOT.

Take a step back though, and behind this seemingly simple pleasure there's a major problem. The dirty secret of the Italian tomato harvest: the 'tomato slaves', paid poverty wages and forced to live in conditions that medical charities have described as 'hellish'.

It is estimated that up to 50,000 migrant workers, many of them illegal immigrants, work in southern Italy's agricultural sector, picking tomatoes, oranges and other fruit. Their temporary homes are often dilapidated shacks, usually without basic services like power or sanitation, with as many as thirty people crowded into a single tiny building: so overcrowded that, whatever the weather, some of them have to sleep outside. Work is a 14-hour day, and what little money they earn is often soaked up by inflated prices charged by gangmasters for accommodation, food or transport. Unable to send money home or even to scrape together enough to leave, this is a life of despair.

Ninety per cent of Italy's annual 4 million tonne tomato harvest is turned into canned tomatoes, purée, paste and passata, or becomes an ingredient in food manufacturing, with more than 80 per cent of the UK's processed tomato imports coming from Italy. You cannot tell whether the tomatoes in a can, or in processed food, were picked by hand or by machine, or what a worker was paid for his labour. And even worse: we know the problem is there, but all the big companies manage to deny any involvement in it. I now try to avoid 'manufactured' baked beans and tomato sauces and make my own, in season, with tomatoes grown locally by people who have been treated with respect, fairness and dignity.

SERVES » 4–6

For the tomato sauce
2 tablespoons olive oil
1 small onion, chopped
2 sticks of celery, diced small
1kg tomatoes, quartered
4 garlic cloves, chopped
2 bay leaves
2 large carrots, diced small
a large handful of fresh oregano
freshly ground black pepper
1 level tablespoon sea salt
For the beans
2 tablespoons olive oil
2 medium onions, finely chopped
1 garlic clove, chopped
600g cooked fava or borlotti beans
700g tomato sauce (see above)
2 tablespoons light muscovado sugar
1 teaspoon five spice powder

Make the sauce in a large heavy-based pan. Heat the oil and sauté the onion, then add the remaining ingredients, cover and reduce the heat to the lowest setting. Leave to cook in its own steam for about 30 minutes, then remove the lid. The mixture will be soft; give it a good stir and cook for a further 3–4 hours, gently bubbling away. Stir occasionally and if it looks like it is catching, add a little water.

Leave until cool enough to handle, then press every last drop through a sieve using a wooden spoon. Discard anything remaining in the sieve. This sauce can be made in large batches and freezes well.

For the beans, heat the oil and sauté the onions and garlic until soft. Add the remaining ingredients to the pan, then bring gently to the boil. Reduce the heat to the lowest setting and simmer for 30 minutes, stirring occasionally. You may need to add a splash of water if the sauce gets too thick.

SHARE WITH FRIENDS PANI PURI

Announcing to dinner guest that they are going to enjoy a sustainable, ethical vegetarian supper can sometimes make guests want to run a mile. There's still the idea that you must be a sandal-wearing, yoga-practising, lentil-munching, Greenpeace-loving environmentalist when you say you care about sustainable food, and while I can't deny that I tick all of the above boxes, I think that in order for a movement to succeed it has to move into the mainstream. To do that means breaking down prejudices and building up a sense of empowerment and belonging. The best way to do that is to share ideas and show people that being a food activist is actually a really delicious and easy thing to incorporate into everyday life. There is no better way of doing this than through food, which is why perhaps this Gujarati-inspired pani puri dish is one of my favourite dishes to make and share. Great food changes attitudes. We put all the bits in the middle of the table and get everyone to build their own. You don't have to stick exactly to the fillings I have used here – my family love to throw a few extra ingredients on the table, so we've been known to add cheese toppings, hummus, guacamole and even leftover salsa. The point is that everyone gets stuck in. It is fun and interactive, and everyone chats, eats, laughs and enjoys, and that is the very best way to face any challenge in life. And before you know it the people who were perhaps sceptical about what being a food activist means are asking questions, and once people start asking questions... well, asking questions is the key to changing the world.

SERVES » 6–8

500g potatoes, cut into 1cm cubes

250g butternut squash, cut into
   1cm cubes

3 tablespoons coconut oil

1 cinnamon stick

3 star anise

½ teaspoon ground cardamom

1 heaped tablespoon mustard seeds

1 tablespoon cumin seeds

2 medium onions, finely chopped

2 tablespoons garam masala

400g can chickpeas, rinsed and drained

150g natural full-fat yogurt

1 teaspoon turmeric

1 teaspoon runny honey

salt and freshly ground black pepper

To serve

45–50 ready-to-eat puris

small bunch of fresh coriander,
   leaves chopped finely

250ml tamarind water

small jar of mango or tamarind chutney

75g sev

Preheat the oven to 180°C/160°C fan/gas 4. Put the potatoes and butternut squash onto baking trays greased with a little of the coconut oil and roast for 6–7 minutes. Turn the vegetables over using a spatula, bake for a further 6–7 minutes, then set aside.

Heat the remaining coconut oil in a large pan then add the cinnamon, star anise, cardamom, mustard and cumin seeds. Stir and cook for 1 minute then add the onions and cook for 2–3 minutes until soft. Add the garam masala, stir well, then add the roasted potatoes, butternut squash and chickpeas. Cook over a medium heat, stirring, for 5–7 minutes then spoon into a serving bowl.

Mix the yogurt, turmeric and honey together in a small bowl, adding salt and black pepper to taste.

Serve the puris, potato filling, flavoured yogurt, coriander, tamarind water, chutney and sev in individual bowls. To assemble, knock a hole gently in the top of a puri and spoon in some potato, a little tamarind water, yogurt and chutney, and sprinkle with coriander and sev.

CLIMATE CHANGE SHELLFISH AND LIME PAELLA

When I got married, it was in Australia, on a beach where the Daintree rainforest meets the Great Barrier Reef. It wasn't a conventional wedding. We had no guests, just a waiter and waitress, who we'd asked to be our witnesses. We said our vows holding hands, sand between our toes, and it was one of the most beautiful moments of my life, as if our promises to each other were witnessed by Nature herself.

The Great Barrier Reef started to grow about 18 million years ago and supports an incredibly diverse range of creatures: not just fish, but whales, dolphins and porpoises, turtles, anemones, sponges and crustaceans, and more than 200 species of bird, which feed on the reef or nest on islands within it. It is, however, under threat. Man-made climate change is warming the oceans, causing a type of degradation known as coral bleaching, which leads to parts of the reef dying off, while overfishing and water pollution have removed natural predators of the Crown of Thorns starfish, which feasts on coral polyps. This in turn had destroyed the habitat and food supply of other marine creatures.

The oceans provide one of the most vital services to our planet: they are natural carbon sinks that absorb CO_2 out of the atmosphere. Yet, as increasing amounts of carbon emissions are released into the atmosphere, we are pushing the capacity of the oceans to act as climate regulators to the limit.

I've used very little meat in this recipe because that's one way to reduce our CO_2 emissions. Sustainably harvested seafood, with generous amounts of organic vegetables and herbs, will still give you a meal to be proud of.

SERVES » 4

2 large pinches of saffron

1 litre hot chicken stock

4 tablespoons olive oil

1 large onion, sliced into rings

4 garlic cloves, finely chopped

1–2 teaspoons Spanish paprika, smoked or picante

150g chorizo, cut into small chunks

400g paella rice

400g can chopped tomatoes

2 bay leaves

For the shellfish

3 tablespoons olive oil

1 garlic clove, peeled and finely chopped

225g cold-water prawns

150g mussels, uncooked

200g clams, uncooked

200g frozen peas

3 limes

freshly ground black pepper

flat-leaf parsley, leaves and stalks finely chopped

If possible, infuse the saffron in the chicken stock overnight, or at least for a few hours before cooking. Heat the olive oil in a large, heavy-based pan and sauté the onion until soft, then add the garlic, paprika and chorizo, and cook for a few minutes more before adding the rice. Turn it in the oil and let it cook for 1–2 minutes before adding the tomatoes, bay leaves and three quarters of the chicken stock. Stir just enough to mix everything, bring to the boil and simmer for 12–15 minutes. If the rice looks dry before it is cooked, add some of the reserved stock, but make sure the result is not sloppy.

Now for the shellfish. In a separate pan, heat the oil, fry the garlic and then sauté the prawns, mussels and clams for 4–5 minutes over a medium heat until cooked.

When the rice is almost cooked, add the shellfish and frozen peas, stir and cook for a further 5 minutes. Then squeeze 2 of the limes and pour their juice over the paella, with a dash more stock or water if it looks dry. Cover with a lid or some foil and set aside for 5 minutes or until the rice has soaked up all the liquid. Serve with a grinding of black pepper and garnish with parsley and the remaining lime cut into wedges.

NO EASY ANSWERS SLOW-ROASTED RED PEPPER QUINOA SALAD

Until a couple of years ago, I'd been merrily eating quinoa believing that it was a fantastic ethical alternative to meat. I was reassured after reading reports confirming its nutritional value as a superfood, and by the UN's Food and Agriculture Organization (FAO) officially declaring 2013 'The International Year of Quinoa'. This was proposed and supported by the governments of Peru and Bolivia (where the plant originated), and quinoa was promoted by the FAO as a food of high nutritive value due to its protein content (14 per cent).

The result? The price of quinoa rocketed and then the *Guardian* ran an article by investigative journalist Joanna Blythman, under the headline 'Can vegans stomach the unpalatable truth about quinoa?'. This made the ethics of eating quinoa seem almost as contentious as eating meat, as she claimed that the price rise fuelled by our enthusiastic consumption had made a staple food of Peru and Bolivia unaffordable to their poorest people. Suddenly, quinoa didn't seem quite so 'super'. In all fairness, I should point out that there were other opinions; for example, that the higher quinoa price lifted many Andean farmers out of poverty, giving them money to spend on education, housing and alternative staple foods, while the Andean Information Network, an NGO active since 1992, said quinoa consumption in Bolivia had been rising. Even the claim that quinoa was now dearer than chicken in Peru's capital, Lima, has to be seen against the fact that in at least one major UK supermarket, a whole free-range chicken costs less per kilo than their cheapest own-label quinoa.

But this uncertainty meant that for ages I threw my hands up in exasperation at the mere mention of this grain. Sometimes there are no easy answers and in the end I came to a compromise. Quinoa is now grown in Shropshire and Essex, and I'll buy local if I feel I'm running up too many food miles. But I also know that if we just stopped buying quinoa from South America, we'd cut off vital income from small farmers. The most effective way to support them is to look for organic quinoa from Peru and Bolivia that is certified fair trade, because that way, we encourage sustainable agriculture and the farmers secure a bigger share of the money generated by world demand for what was once their simple staple food.

SERVES » 6

- 4–5 large red peppers, deseeded and sliced
- 3 red or green chillies, deseeded
- 4 medium onions, sliced
- 60ml olive oil
- 500g quinoa
- 1 teaspoon sea salt
- 60g pumpkin seeds
- a handful of parsley, chopped
- juice of 1 lime
- 100g fresh pomegranate seeds
- 2 teaspoons sumac
- 1–2 tablespoons pomegranate juice or pomegranate molasses

Preheat the oven to 170°C/150°C fan/gas 3. Put the red peppers, chillies and onions on a baking tray, drizzle with the olive oil and slow roast for 30 minutes. Leave to cool.

Meanwhile, put the quinoa and salt in a pan with about 1.5 litres of cold water, cover and bring to the boil. Reduce the temperature and simmer for 15 minutes. If the pot looks like it is running dry, add a little more water. Tip into a serving dish to cool.

Fold the roasted vegetables, pumpkin seeds, parsley and lime juice into the quinoa. Scatter with the pomegranate seeds and sumac, drizzle the pomegranate juice over the top and serve.

A BETTER LIFE PERFECT ROAST CHICKEN

Roast chicken is like a magnet, drawing people in, as garlicky lemon and thyme wafts escape from the kitchen. I never have to call the family to eat, because everyone is already milling about close to the oven long before I am ready to serve. Inevitably, one of my children wants to pick at the caramelised sticky bits at the bottom of the pan that I need to make utterly delicious gravy. In our house, roast chicken has to be served with dollops of mashed potato and garlicky green beans, and life is good.

The question is though... was life good for the chicken? We know that intensively farmed birds don't have much of a life. Most of the 17 million chickens sold each week in the UK go at breakneck speed from 0–6 weeks, through the factory farm and into the cellophane wrapper. I spoke to investigative food journalist Andrew Wasley, who has made several documentaries about intensive farming, and asked him what life is like for the birds. 'Many factory farms are huge, the size of football pitches, and if people could see inside they'd be both shocked and appalled. It's hot and stuffy and the atmosphere is dusty. It stinks of ammonia, there is no daylight and no floor space. The birds are almost unrecognisable if compared to our romantic images of farmyard chickens. The truth is that they are miserable-looking creatures, often caked in faeces.'

I can't eat a bird that's lived a life like that; yes, it is more expensive to buy organic free-range poultry, but the more I've read about the reality of intensive farming, the more uncomfortable I have become with the moral cost of cheap chicken. So the perfect roast chicken... starts with a free-range chicken.

SERVES » 6

1.6kg chicken
2 bay leaves
a handful of lemon thyme
5–6 garlic cloves
zest and juice of 2 lemons
3 tablespoons olive oil
2 teaspoons sea salt
140ml white wine
½ teaspoon fair trade sugar
2–3 tablespoons cornflour
30ml single cream (optional)

Preheat the oven to 240°C/220°C fan/gas 9. Put the chicken in a roasting tin. Hold the chicken cavity open and place the bay leaves, thyme, garlic and lemon zest inside the bird and under the skin covering the breast. Drizzle over the oil and sprinkle the salt over the top of the chicken. Reduce the oven temperature to 200°C/180°C fan/gas 6 and roast the chicken for 1 hour.

Baste the chicken with the juices from the pan and add the wine. After a further 20 minutes, check that the chicken is done by inserting a skewer into the thigh and making sure that the juices run clear. If they are still pink, return the chicken to the oven for a further 10 minutes and repeat the test.

Remove the chicken from the roasting tin and set aside. A few minutes' rest are important in order to allow the meat to relax – it will be much more tender as a result.

Strain the cooking liquor into a gravy separator if you have one, returning the juices to the pan, or carefully skim the fat off with a spoon. Over a medium heat, add the lemon juice and stir in the sugar. You can add more or less sugar or some salt and black pepper, depending on taste.

In a small bowl, mix the cornflour to a thin paste with a little cold water. Add it to the pan while stirring, over a medium heat, to thicken the gravy. It is best to cook this through for a minute or so. For a more voluptuous sauce, stir in the cream just before serving.

THINK AHEAD MOROCCAN ROAST CHICKEN with couscous

This North African-inspired chicken dish makes an easy and delicious family supper, with something to spare for tomorrow's packed lunch. When you are hungry and short of time at work, convictions about eating in the most considered way possible can suddenly feel inconvenient. It can be hard to find something to eat that is ethically produced and sustainably grown, amongst all the processed, cheap convenience foods and special offers. Thinking ahead and taking control of your food puts you firmly in charge. It gives you the opportunity to source your meat and to use garden herbs, pesticide-free vegetables and fairly traded spices. Making extra in your evening meal is no effort and really avoids testing your willpower the following day.

If you don't plan ahead, be aware that that it's not just that most meat used in convenience food is factory-farmed. The chicken salad sandwich on sale in one British supermarket contains chicken from Brazil or Thailand, steam-cooked with added cornflour and manufactured in the Republic of Ireland before being sent here for sale. I don't need my lunch to carry that many food miles or that ethical burden. I can take the Royal Society for the Prevention of Cruelty to Animals' (RSPCA) advice and look for a Freedom Food, organic or free-range label; or I can go that bit further and make active choices about starting to change the system. And choices mean planning.

SERVES » 6

For the chicken

1.6kg chicken

2 bay leaves

5 garlic cloves, peeled

finely grated zest and juice of
    2 unwaxed lemons

3 tablespoons olive or rapeseed oil

2 teaspoons sea salt

4 tablespoons ras el hanout

3 x 400g cans chopped tomatoes

½ teaspoon brown sugar

For the couscous

500g couscous

1 teaspoon sea salt

100g sultanas

a handful of chopped fresh mint

45g unsalted butter, softened

40g flaked almonds, toasted

Preheat the oven to 240°C/220°C fan/gas 9. Put the bay leaves, garlic and lemon zest inside the cavity of the chicken, then place the chicken in a deep casserole dish with a well-fitting lid or a large tagine. Rub the skin of the chicken with the oil, then sprinkle with salt and ras el hanout. Place the dish into the oven, uncovered, then reduce the heat to 200°C/180°C fan/gas 6 and roast for 30 minutes.

Next, baste the chicken with the juices from the bottom of the pan. Add the tomatoes and sugar then bake for a further hour with the lid on. To check that the chicken is cooked, insert a skewer in the thigh and make sure that the juices run clear. If they are still pink, return the chicken to the oven for a further 10 minutes and repeat the test.

Remove the chicken from the dish and set aside to rest for 20 minutes – the meat will be much more tender if you do.

Meanwhile, make the couscous according to the instructions on the packet. Season with the sea salt and stir in the sultanas, mint, butter and the lemon juice, fluffing with a fork. Transfer to a warmed serving dish and scatter with the toasted almonds.

Serve immediately with the warm chicken and some of the tomato sauce from the cooking dish. To provide packed lunches for the next day, cut some of the chicken into individual portions and when cold, refrigerate with a little sauce spooned over and a helping of the couscous (excellent with a spoonful of dip, see page 114).

RARE BREED ROAST BEEF

A properly matured joint of beef is a thing of beauty. Dark marbled flesh, with cream-coloured fat that will baste the meat as it roasts gently, with nothing but a little seasoning, in a slow oven. As the fat melts and puckers, and the meat cooks until it is tender, the house fills with an almost primitive smell of roasting meat.

There are those who simply buy meat that's cheap or convenient, who never look past the shrink-wrap. It is just another product and they don't want to make a connection from the packet to the animal. Then there are those whose concerns about the politics of food have led them to renounce meat or to eat it guiltily. There is, however, a space in between for the consumer who wants to eat meat that contributes to sustainability. One way of doing this is to buy meat from rare breeds of livestock, which are under serious threat of disappearing.

If we lose our rare breeds, we don't just lose biodiversity. We lose robust, hardy animal types that have in many cases been developed over hundreds of years to survive and thrive on relatively marginal land. These are breeds that don't gain weight as fast, or grow as large, as the hybrid cattle popular in intensive beef farming, and that don't have the huge milk yields of modern dairy cattle (a Shetland cow might give on average 12 litres a day, compared to a Holstein/Friesian cross producing possibly 22 litres). But equally, they don't develop any of the physical problems which over-stretched dairy cattle can experience, or need their food constantly supplemented in order to achieve growth targets. And because they are rare breeds, they are usually raised by a different type of farmer. One who will use sustainable, organic and animal-friendly farming practices, be personally concerned about animal welfare, and in many cases, use a smaller local abbatoir and butcher, which means that at the end of their lives, their cattle have a better quality of death: spared the auction process, long road journey, and the stress of an industrial slaughterhouse. And quite simply: the meat tastes better, too.

SERVES » 6

2–3kg rib joint (3–4 ribs)
sea salt and freshly ground black pepper
10–12 beef marrowbone pieces,
    cut lengthways
1 red onion, thinly sliced
6–8 anchovy fillets, roughly chopped
2 teaspoons lemon juice
small bunch of fresh dill, chopped
sourdough toast, to serve

For the Homemade Beef Gravy
400–500ml water
sprig of rosemary
4–5 tablespoons redcurrant, quince or
    crab apple jelly (page 203)
2 heaped tablespoons cornflour mixed
    with 6–8 tablespoons cold water
salt and freshly ground black pepper

Heat the oven to 220°C/200°C fan/gas 7. Season the beef well with salt and black pepper, place it in a large roasting tin and roast for 30 minutes, then reduce the temperature to 160°C/140°C fan/gas 2½. Cook for 20 minutes per 450g for medium, or 15 minutes per 450g for rare.

About 30 minutes before the end of cooking, add the beef marrowbones to the roasting tin, cut-side upwards, along with the onion and anchovies.

When the cooking time is up, let the beef stand for 20 minutes before serving on a carving dish. Transfer the bones onto a platter, and keep warm. Just before serving them, sprinkle with the lemon juice, dill and a little more salt, and make sure everyone has a small spoon so they can scrape out the marrow onto some hot sourdough toast.

HOMEMADE BEEF GRAVY

When your beef joint is cooked, remove the meat and bones from the pan, leaving the onion and anchovy fillets with the juices. Holding one corner of the roasting tin with a tea towel, tip it gently to drain off almost all the fat into a bowl, removing the last of it with a large spoon. Put the roasting tin over a high heat, add the water and rosemary and bring to the boil, scraping the pan to release any baked-on bits. Stir in the jelly, followed by the cornflour liquid, and bring to the boil. Reduce, if necessary, to the desired thickness. Season, and strain into a serving jug.

SMALLER FOOTPRINT VEGAN DAL

Dal is the name for both the dried split lentil and the thick, soupy stew made from it, which is a staple part of the diet of hundreds of millions of people across Nepal, India, Pakistan and Bangladesh. As *dal bhat* – literally lentils and rice – it provides both starch and protein in a diet that contains little or no meat. You can have it on the table in less time than it takes for a takeaway ordered over the phone to arrive, and aside from the fact that it costs very little to make, it helps the planet too. The United Nation's Food and Agriculture Organization estimates that animals bred and killed for food generate about 18 per cent of the world's greenhouse gas emissions, which is more than the entire transport sector, so having one more meat-free dinner each week will help to reduce your personal 'footprint'.

This was the very first 'Indian' dish I made when I went to university. I really didn't have a clue what I was doing, but Raj, the owner of a corner shop on Belgrave Road in Leicester, translated as an elderly Gujarati lady talked me through the basics. She put various ingredients in my basket, none of which had names I understood, and I cycled home and made dal. I was so proud, and I have been making it ever since. A family friend from Nepal later showed me how to use coconut oil in this recipe instead of ghee, which makes it a vegan dish. It's really easy to make, and will give you a wonderful fragrant and filling simple meal.

SERVES » 4–6

3 tablespoons coconut oil

2 medium onions, finely chopped

3 tablespoons garam masala

finely grated zest of 1 lime

finely grated zest of 1 lemon

250g red lentils

approx. 650ml cold water

1 level tablespoon sea salt

1 tablespoon jaggery or dark brown sugar

For the topping

2 tablespoons coconut oil

1 tablespoon fennel seeds

1 tablespoon coriander seeds

1 tablespoon cumin seeds

a handful of fresh coriander, leaves only,
   roughly chopped

Put the coconut oil in a large heavy pan over a moderate heat then add the onions and sauté until lightly golden. Stir in the garam masala and lime and lemon zests, cook for a further minute then add the lentils and water and bring to the boil. Reduce the heat, cover the pan, then simmer for 20–25 minutes until the lentils are soft. Check and stir often to make sure they do not dry out, adding more water if necessary. You want the dal consistency to be somewhere between a purée and very thick soup. Stir in the sugar and salt just before serving.

Meanwhile, make the aromatic topping. Heat the coconut oil in a separate pan, add the fennel, coriander and cumin seeds and cook for about 2 minutes until the oil is fragrant. Set aside. When the dal is ready to serve, pour the spiced coconut oil over the top, and sprinkle with the fresh coriander.

Perfect served with steamed or boiled long-grain or basmati rice and a spoonful of spicy pickle.

SAVE THE SOIL PUMPKIN AND CHICKPEA CURRY

This curry is dark, spicy, soft and earthy. It's also meat-free, with the chickpeas providing protein. Serving organic yogurt with it cuts the richness with just a mild acidity, and gives you a healthy hit of lactic bacteria: great for your stomach. Patrick Holden of the Sustainable Food Trust describes soil as 'the stomach of the plant' because it is home to a complex system of helpful bacterial and fungal microorganisms: the 'feeding mechanism' of the plant itself. But this depends on a healthy layer of topsoil, and the problem is that soil erosion and degradation is the global environmental threat that we're not talking about.

Globally, 40 per cent of land used for agriculture is either degraded or seriously degraded, because topsoil is being lost. Over time, intensive use of chemical fertilisers and 'modern' farming techniques strip the soil of carbon and nutrients, reducing soil fertility. In many places, it is also destroying the ability of the soil to retain water, which washes straight through and isn't absorbed by plant root systems.

Don't imagine that this is just a problem for countries far away, and that we will be unaffected. Soil erosion and failed irrigation will lead to crises and conflicts caused by shortages of both food and water. This won't just mean more requests for humanitarian aid, it will mean more 'failed states', more civil unrest, and more opportunities for despots to cause terror, within their own countries and across borders. It will also mean more refugees, desperately seeking food and safety.

We have to stop subsidising unsustainable farming systems that are costing us our planet, and instead reward those who produce food that supports the health of our soil and thus the health of society. This is why it matters when you shop for your family. Look for organic, fair trade produce. Eat less meat. Buy ingredients that have been grown by sustainable methods that look after the soil. At the 'micro' level, try to generate less food waste, and if you can, ensure that peelings and offcuts end up in the compost, not going to landfill.

SERVES » 4

50ml chilli oil, maybe a little more

1 tablespoon mustard seeds

3 star anise

5 whole green cardamom pods

1 cinnamon stick

2 red onions, sliced

¼ small pumpkin, peeled, deseeded, and cut into 2cm chunks

3 heaped tablespoons garam masala

pinch of salt

400g can chickpeas, drained and rinsed

1 tablespoon date syrup

3 tablespoons natural yogurt, plus extra to serve

small bunch of fresh coriander, chopped

In a deep pan, heat the chilli oil then add the mustard seeds, star anise, cardamom and cinnamon. Cook gently for 2 minutes or until the mustard seeds stop popping. Add the onions and cook for about 5 minutes until just beginning to turn golden. Add the pumpkin and cook over a low heat for 8–10 minutes; if it starts to catch, add a little more oil. Add the garam masala and salt, along with 2–3 tablespoons of cold water. Continue to cook over a medium–low heat. Stir in the chickpeas, and as the curry cooks and begins to dry out, add a couple tablespoons of water at a time if needed, so that the curry remains moist and doesn't catch on the pan. Cook for a further 15 minutes until the pumpkin is soft and cooked through.

Pick the star anise, cardamom and cinnamon out of the pan. Remove from the heat, leave to cool for 5 minutes, then add the date syrup and yogurt, and check for seasoning. Sprinkle with the coriander. Serve with basmati rice and a bowl of organic natural yogurt.

IN FROM THE COLD KING PRAWN TIKKA MASALA

When Hugh Fearnley-Whittingstall said 'king prawns are the "battery chickens" of the fish world', it sounded dramatic, but as I love eating prawns, I decided to investigate further. Tropical prawns are farmed in salt-water ponds, often created by destroying vast areas of mangrove forest which had protected coastal communities from tsunamis, tidal surges and tropical storms. To feed the prawns, thousands of tonnes of fish are caught illegally in marine nature reserves, to be processed into fishmeal. Investigations over the past decade have unveiled human rights abuses linking over 150 violent deaths to the prawn industry in Bangladesh and other countries. From beatings at protests against land-grabbing by big companies in coastal areas, to slave labour conditions for migrant workers and on to murder; this leaves me in no doubt that the tropical prawn industry is often a dirty business. When I asked award-winning investigative journalist Andrew Wasley, who has made several documentaries about intensive prawn farming, about sustainable king prawns, his response was unequivocal: 'I've been researching the industry for over a decade, and I've never seen a truly ethical or sustainably produced "tropical" prawn. I have to doubt even those that claim sustainability, because the true cost of prawn production is well hidden'.

Make this dish using sustainably caught cold-water prawns, ideally from fisheries in the north-east Arctic and Canada. They may not be quite as big, but you'll be able to avoid your dinner leaving a nasty taste in your mouth.

SERVES » 4

For the marinated prawns
200g full-fat yogurt
1 tablespoon freshly grated ginger
1 tablespoon freshly grated garlic
1 teaspoon ground coriander
½ teaspoon garam masala
1 tablespoon rapeseed oil
1 tablespoon lemon juice
½ tablespoon gram flour (chickpea flour)
500g raw, peeled cold-water king
   prawns, thawed

For the tikka masala
2 tablespoons rapeseed oil
2 cloves
2 black or green cardamom pods
1 bay leaf
1 onion, finely chopped
5cm piece of fresh root ginger, grated
1 teaspoon ground cumin
1 teaspoon ground coriander
½ teaspoon red chilli powder
200g canned chopped tomatoes
1 large tablespoon mango chutney
   (liquid part only)
150ml coconut milk
sea salt and freshly ground black pepper
1 teaspoon garam masala
a handful of finely chopped coriander
   leaves
4 tablespoons double cream

Mix all the ingredients for the marinade together in a large bowl, then add the prawns. Stir to coat, then cover and refrigerate for a minimum of 2 hours and preferably 8 hours.

To make the tikka masala, heat the oil in a large pan and sauté the cloves, cardamom and bay leaf for 1 minute then add the onion and ginger. Sauté for 5–7 minutes until the onion is translucent. Strain the prawns, discarding the marinade, add them to the pan and sauté for 2–3 minutes, just until the prawns are pink and cooked through.

Add the ground cumin and coriander, and the chilli powder and sauté the mixture for 2–3 minutes more, then add the tomatoes. Stir well for a few minutes, then add the mango chutney and coconut milk. Stir the mixture well.

Season with salt and black pepper, then sprinkle over the garam masala and coriander. Stir in the cream and serve with rice, parathas or naan bread.

RICE FARMERS' SPECIAL FRIED RICE

Friday night is takeaway night. It's the end of a long working week and there are times, even for people who love nothing more than to cook, when dialling for a take-out is about as much effort as you can manage. But before you reach for the phone, take a few seconds and ask yourself this: how hard did the people who grew and picked the rice that you are about to eat work? And were they paid a fair price? While you are wondering about the farmers that grew the rice, it's worth asking where the prawns came from too (see page 85).

More than 1 billion people – predominantly small farmers in developing countries – earn their living from rice production. But across the world, they are being squeezed from all directions. Subsidised rice from wealthier nations is dumped onto international markets, while the cost of fertiliser escalates, leaving farmers trapped between lower prices and higher costs.

Buying fair trade rice helps small farmers live a life with a little more hope and dignity. Through forming cooperatives within their communities, they can sell what they grow at an agreed minimum price. They're also able to access external advice and expertise, to help them use agrochemicals more economically, and to move towards sustainable husbandry. The fair trade premium also means that villages can invest in social projects, providing things we simply take for granted, such as schools and basic health services... and there is no child labour. Now think about that for a moment.

My children go to school. They play when they are not in school and when they are ill they see a doctor. I'd like that to be every child's right. So no matter how tempting it is to phone for a takeaway, the reality is that our daily decisions have an impact on the hopes and dreams of real families on the other side of the world; by using fair trade rice, you help them take one step in a positive direction.

The rice you use for this recipe needs to be cooked, cold and dry, to stop it sticking.

SERVES 4–6

4 tablespoons rapeseed oil
2 onions, very finely chopped
2 garlic cloves, finely chopped
2.5cm piece of fresh root ginger, finely grated
1 fresh red chilli, finely chopped
500g cooked long-grain rice, cold
2 tablespoons sesame oil
4 tablespoons soy sauce
3 spring onions, cut into 3mm rings
3 medium eggs, beaten with a pinch of white pepper
200g frozen peas, thawed and drained
150g prawns, cooked
a handful of freshly chopped coriander

Heat a large wok until it is very hot. Add the rapeseed oil and then the onions and fry for 1 minute, stirring constantly, before adding the garlic, ginger and two thirds of the chilli (reserve the remainder to garnish).

Continue stirring, with the wok over a high heat, and add the cooked rice, a few tablespoons at a time. Fry for about 5 minutes, then add the sesame oil and soy sauce, followed by the spring onions.

Add the beaten eggs, drizzling them quickly across the rice so they don't form one large lump, and stir furiously to coat the rice. Finally, add the peas and prawns, and quickly stir one last time.

Serve immediately scattered with the coriander and the reserved fresh chilli.

PORK NEEDS PROVENANCE CHINESE-STYLE DUMPLINGS

Cloudless blue skies, a frosty morning and dry twigs that snap underfoot, air so cold I can see my breath dancing in front of me as I walk. Clear, dry winter days are my favourites. They are 'bowls of sweet-spiced warm Chinese dumplings' days.

What doesn't warm my heart is the knowledge that industrial pig farming systems are abusive: the animals never see the light of day and are kept on concrete floors under fluorescent lights, in such cramped conditions that they barely have room to turn around. Terms meant to sell us the idea of decent animal welfare, like 'outdoor bred', can disguise the less bucolic truth that the piglets only lived outside for their first four weeks of life and were then intensively reared indoors, just as 'outdoor reared' may still mean confinement to tents or sheds with little scope for natural pig behaviour. Free-range pork is the most ethical choice, and buying from your local butcher means you can support a small farmer and an independent retailer, and ensures that the meat you're eating came from a pig that had a better quality of life. If you can't find free range, look for higher animal welfare pork, such as pigs reared in low-density, deep-straw bedded indoor systems.

This recipe is for the dumpling filling and dipping sauce. I buy the wrappers as they are neatly rolled and contain little more than flour, water, egg and salt.

MAKES »40 DUMPLINGS

For the dipping sauce

4 tablespoons soy sauce

1½ teaspoons runny honey

2 garlic cloves, finely chopped

1 small red chilli, deseeded and
finely chopped

2 small spring onions, finely chopped

2 tablespoons sesame seed oil

2 teaspoons Shaoxing rice wine or
sweet sherry

For the filling

450g minced pork

1 medium egg, beaten

2 teaspoons sesame seed oil

5–7.5cm piece of fresh root ginger,
peeled and very finely grated

4 spring onions, very finely chopped

1 teaspoon Chinese five spice powder

2 tablespoons dark soy sauce

1 tablespoon runny honey

2 small chillies, deseeded and
finely chopped

2 x 200g packets (about 30 sheets
each) of wonton wrappers (better
to have more than you need)

rice flour, for dusting

To make the dipping sauce, put all the ingredients together in a bowl and mix well. Put all the filling ingredients (minus the wrappers and rice flour) in a large bowl and mix well with your hands. Refrigerate for 12 hours for a more intense flavour (if you are in a hurry, you can make the dumplings immediately).

Have a small dish of cold water ready. Lay 12 wonton wrappers on a work surface. Place 1 teaspoon of filling in the centre of each wrapper, then dip a finger into the water and run it over the clean edges of the pastry. Fold each wrapper over into a triangle and press gently around the edges to seal. Transfer to a tray lightly dusted with rice flour. Repeat until all the pork filling is used up (you can freeze the dumplings and any leftover wrappers at this point).

Bring a large pan of salted water to the boil. Drop in 7–8 dumplings at a time and boil for 2 minutes, then remove with a slotted spoon. Drain and repeat until they are all cooked. Serve with the dipping sauce on the side or spoon a little over each helping.

If you are cooking these from frozen, allow an extra minute's cooking time.

FAST LANE TO EXTINCTION SLOW-COOKED PORK SHOULDER

I'm always reluctant to eat meat if I don't know its provenance, and I don't cook it every day, because of its carbon footprint. When I do have it, it's locally reared and it has to taste good. A rubbing paste makes this pork really special.

Soy sauce is one of the most popular and instantly recognisable flavours from Asian cuisine. Unfortunately, it is made from a fermented paste of boiled soya beans, a crop which in South America is linked to the loss of rainforest and savannah, and with it the habitat of many endangered species. Soil erosion, water pollution from the run-off of chemical fertilisers and pesticides are follow-on problems, and what was a thriving rainforest can rapidly become poisoned land.

Soya beans are processed into animal feed, in particular for industrial-scale indoor farming of poultry and pork. They are also an ingredient in a huge range of processed (human) foods and are refined into vegetable oil. Most of the crop is now genetically modified, to give it immunity to glyphosate weedkiller; and commonly in South America, farmers spray the fields with massive quantities of this herbicide throughout the growing season. Parallel to this change, doctors report massively higher rates of miscarriages, birth defects and childhood cancers in nearby rural communities.

Recently, a report presented by Professor Paul Ehrlich of Stanford University told us that 'without any significant doubt we are now entering the sixth great mass extinction', with species disappearing at one hundred times the normal rate. The cause? Human impact, including forest clearance for farming, carbon emissions driving climate change and ocean acidification, and the use of toxic chemicals that poison ecosystems. The warning is that without determined efforts to change course, humans will also become extinct. So what I'm going to use here is a recipe that a friend gave me, for a soy sauce substitute. Choose your pork wisely and you can have a soya-free dinner.

SERVES » 6

For the soy sauce substitute
4 teaspoons black treacle
2 tablespoons balsamic vinegar
2 teaspoons cider vinegar
250ml beef stock
good pinch of garlic powder
good pinch of ground white pepper
½ teaspoon ground ginger
½ teaspoon salt
1 teaspoon fish sauce

For the pork
2 tablespoons soy sauce substitute
1 bulb garlic, finely chopped
6cm piece of fresh root ginger, peeled and finely grated
1 tablespoon rice wine
1 tablespoon sesame oil
3½ tablespoons sesame seeds
50g runny honey
1½ tablespoons five spice powder
1 level tablespoon cornflour (optional)
2kg pork shoulder joint

For the soy sauce substitute, put the black treacle, both vinegars, beef stock, garlic powder and ground spices in a pan and bring to the boil, then reduce the heat to a simmer and cook for about 10 minutes until reduced by half. Remove from the heat, stir in the salt and fish sauce and check the taste; add more seasoning if you want. Pour into a sterilised glass jar or bottle, cover and leave to cool. Store in the fridge for 7–14 days.

Preheat the oven to 220°C/200°C fan/gas 7. In a large bowl, mix the 'soy', garlic, ginger, rice wine, sesame oil and seeds, honey and five spice together to make the rubbing paste. Thicken with cornflour if needed. Coat the pork evenly with the paste, then place it on a rack in a roasting tin. Pour 125ml of cold water into the bottom of the tin, cover tightly with foil and put into the oven. Reduce the temperature to 120°C/100°C fan/gas ½ and cook for 6–8 hours, or until the pork is tender and falling off the bone.

DEMAND CHANGE NOODLES

I first enjoyed noodles topped with chopped cashew nuts in Vietnam, and viewed them as an innocent pleasure: just a bowl of warming food, filled with sweet, salty, spicy flavours. Back in the UK, cashews were being promoted as a healthy option, rich in minerals and soluble dietary fibre, and full of 'heart-friendly' monounsaturated fatty acids: the ideal snack food. I think that if I had known then what I know now, I would have spat those nuts out in disgust; two newspaper articles told me things I'd never known about the appalling conditions of many farmers and workers in the cashew industry.

Cashew trees bear a 'pseudofruit' called the cashew apple, and the 'nut' is actually an external seed, carried underneath the fruit in a double shell. That shell contains a resinous substance, anarcardic acid, which is a potent skin irritant, similar to that found in the cashew's relative, poison ivy. And that's the problem: shelling is a labour-intensive process, carried out by poorly paid workers in countries like India and Vietnam. Latex gloves, which would protect their hands, are frequently not provided by employers, and permanent skin damage is seen as an occupational hazard. Even the initial roasting carried out to loosen the shells releases noxious fumes containing droplets of the irritant, which if inhaled can cause life-threatening lung problems.

What I found when I looked further confirmed my suspicion that it is not just women but children who are working in the cashew nut industry, but the horror doesn't stop there. Vietnam is the world's largest exporter of processed cashews, and *Time* magazine reported that drug addicts detained in rehab centres are forced to perform 'labour therapy' shelling cashews, with beatings, electric shocks and food deprivation if they refuse.

Fair trade cashews are available, if you look; more often, the packaging simply states the country of origin, with no commitment to people's welfare. But we can change things. We need to shame the companies that supply these nuts. Complain to customer services that you are disgusted by what their packaging hides. Find their Facebook page, link to the article mentioned above. Ask your MP to raise the question of why these imports are allowed. And when you shop for this recipe, look again at exactly what you are buying.

SERVES » 4

260g 'ribbon' rice noodles

4–5 tablespoons sesame oil

2 tablespoons sunflower oil

2 small red onions, finely sliced

2 small courgettes, finely sliced

1 medium red pepper, finely sliced

4 garlic cloves, finely sliced

2 tablespoons soy sauce

juice of 1 lime

2 tablespoons fish sauce

4cm piece of fresh root ginger, peeled and finely grated

2 tablespoons runny honey

60g cashew nuts, chopped

small bunch of fresh coriander, finely chopped

Cook the noodles according to the packet instructions, then refresh under cold running water, drain, and drizzle with 1–2 tablespoons of the sesame oil to prevent them sticking. Set aside.

Heat the sunflower oil in a large wok. Add the onions and cook for 1 minute, then add the courgettes and red pepper; cook for a further minute. Add the garlic and cook until it smells aromatic, about 1 minute.

Throw in the cooked noodles and stir gently, then add the soy sauce, lime juice, remaining sesame oil, fish sauce, ginger and honey. Cook for 2 minutes over a medium heat.

Tip into a serving dish and top with the cashews and coriander. This dish is delicious served either hot or cold.

POLYSTYRENE-FREE FISH AND CHIPS

I love really great fish and chips. But if it comes served in a polystyrene cone, or a foam tray with plastic cutlery, my feeling of bliss disappears, even if the food is sensationally good. What's wrong with old-fashioned paper?

I don't want to eat off the very thing we are polluting the oceans with: plastic and polystyrene. A report presented in 2009 to the American Chemical Society reminded us that while we see plastic products as physically stable, plastic in the ocean decomposes as it is exposed to rain, sun and other environmental conditions, causing contamination on a global scale. Even worse, toxic substances released from decomposing plastic are absorbed by marine life forms in a way that doesn't naturally happen if undecayed plastic is eaten by land animals.

While we wait for a solution to the problem of plastic in our oceans, we can decide not to do anything that makes it worse. Avoid using polystyrene and disposable plastics wherever possible, and encourage your local chippy to go back to wrapping everything in paper or to use biodegradable containers. Many already do, and supporting them is the way forward. Or, when you have the time and want a comforting supper, make your own fish and chips, served on proper china plates.

The traditional dried marrowfat peas needed for proper mushy peas are often missing from my local shop, so what I've done here is give you my recipe for 'crushy' peas, using organic frozen peas, which may be easier to find.

SERVES » 4

For the 'crushy' peas
600g frozen peas
large knob of butter, approx.
    2 tablespoons
juice of 1 lemon
sea salt and freshly ground black pepper
a small handful of fresh mint leaves
olive oil, to serve

For the fish
approx. 800g skinless and boneless
    haddock, hake or cod fillet
3 tablespoons plain flour
pinch of salt

For frying and for the batter
650ml sunflower oil
1 egg white
125ml ice-cold sparkling cider
65g self-raising flour
65g cornflour
sea salt and freshly ground black pepper

Put the frozen peas in a pan with the butter, lemon juice, salt and half the mint, saving the rest for garnish. Cover and cook over a medium heat for 8–10 minutes, stirring frequently, adding a little water if needed to stop them sticking. Mash roughly and keep warm until served.

Cut the fish into individual portions. Mix the flour and salt on a plate and coat each fillet evenly.

Meanwhile, heat the oil in a deep plain metal pan to approx. 200°C. The oil should come to no more than one third the way up the side of the pan, which must not be non-stick.

Make the batter by whisking the egg white in a large mixing bowl until fluffy. Then add half the cider with the flour, cornflour, and salt and black pepper. Mix very lightly to keep the bubbles in the mixture, then stir in the remaining cider. Dip two fish fillets into the batter and lower them into the hot oil using a slotted metal spoon. Cook for 5–6 minutes until golden, turning once to make sure both sides are cooked evenly. Drain the fish on a tray lined with kitchen paper and keep warm; check the oil temperature is still 200°C then repeat with the remaining fillets.

Serve with the 'crushy' peas garnished with a drizzle of olive oil, a grinding of black pepper and the remaining mint scattered on top. Great with Homemade and Heritage Oven-baked Chips (page 137).

AND ONE FOR LATER
WILD BOAR SALAMI AND ROCKET PIZZA

Like most people, I want a pizza once in a while. I suppose there's a certain irony in the fact that the time I most want it is definitely not when I have the energy to make it, which can make ethical choices more difficult. I've bought supermarket pizzas, but they often seem a poor substitute for homemade, and while I'm not going to denounce all takeaway pizzas, they are getting more and more expensive. So the answer I've come up with is to make two pizzas when I have the time, freezing one for later.

This recipe uses local organic flour, organic yeast and outdoor-reared wild boar salami. I am not going to pretend that the salami isn't expensive, but you only need a small amount and it still works out cheaper than a large pizza from my local delivery company. It tastes amazing, and wild boar meat is leaner than pork and full of amino-acids. If you want the most sustainable pizza, make it vegetarian; I'm married to a dedicated carnivore, so this recipe is for him.

MAKES ▸ 2x30cm PIZZAS

For the dough
5g dried yeast
350ml tepid water
500g strong white flour, plus extra
    for dusting
100g finely ground semolina flour,
    plus extra for baking
10g fine sea salt
2 tablespoons olive oil, for kneading
For the pizza sauce
2 tablespoons olive oil
2 garlic cloves, finely chopped
2 bay leaves
2 x 400g cans chopped tomatoes
1 teaspoon sea salt
For the topping
240g mozzarella-style cheese
240g local soft goat's cheese
200g wild boar salami
a large handful of rocket, fresh oregano
    leaves and chilli oil, to serve

Put the yeast into a jug and add 100ml of the water. Whisk and set aside somewhere warm for 10 minutes. Weigh the flour, semolina and salt in a large bowl and make a well in the centre. Add the yeasty liquid with the remaining water. Mix until all the flour is incorporated, then cover and leave for 10 minutes. Turn the dough onto a lightly oiled surface and knead well for 5 minutes. Return the dough to the bowl, cover with a clean, damp tea towel and set aside somewhere warm for 1½–2 hours.

To make the sauce, heat the oil in a heavy-based pan. Lightly sauté the garlic, and add the bay leaves, tomatoes and salt. Bring to the boil; reduce the heat to a very low simmer, stirring occasionally for about 1 hour, until reduced at least by half. Set aside to cool.

With a baking stone on the middle shelf, preheat the oven to 230°C/210°C fan/gas 8. On a floured surface, divide the dough in half and lightly shape into balls. Using your fingertips, press each ball out into a circle, then stretch gently with your hands to make 30cm-diameter bases.

Dust a large, flat, upside-down baking tray with semolina, and, using a rolling pin, lift one base onto it. Carefully cover with half the sauce, cheeses and salami. Slide this quickly but carefully onto the hot baking stone and bake for 10–12 minutes; check and bake a little more if necessary. Leave to cool a little, before serving with a scattering of rocket, oregano and a drizzle of chilli oil.

Meanwhile, transfer the other pizza to a baking tray lined with greaseproof paper and sprinkled with semolina. Add the sauce and toppings (minus the rocket). Put this in the freezer for 4–5 hours. Once frozen, wrap with a second layer of greaseproof paper and store inside a bag, to prevent freezer burn (I keep mine in an old supermarket bag). Bake for slightly longer from frozen. You can freeze the base with just sauce on it, and add the toppings when you bake it.

ETHICAL BARBECUED LAMB IN PITTA BREAD

For an instant festive atmosphere nothing beats a barbecue. The sun is shining, and being British, well, we'll barbecue at the mere suggestion of sunshine. But the big question is: how do we have a guilt-free, ethical barbecue?

The question of climate change hangs over the topic like a great black cloud. A 2014 report from the Centre for Ecology and Hydrology pointed out that if everyone in the European Union halved their meat and dairy consumption it would reduce EU greenhouse gas emissions from agriculture by 25–40 per cent and nitrogen emissions by 40 per cent, and the EU could become a major exporter of food products, instead of an importer of, for example, soya beans, which are used almost exclusively for animal feed. This doesn't mean going hungry: it does mean eating more cereals, lentils, beans and other vegetables. Not full vegetarianism, but what's been called a demitarian diet, which would still provide us with more protein than our bodies actually need.

A gentle first step towards this is to buy less meat but more locally reared lamb – one of the few farm animals that is nearly always grass fed – and bulk your meal out with more vegetables, fruit, pulses and salad. Barbecuing has evolved from an eat-as-much-meat-as-you-can fest to a far more sophisticated meal, celebrated by incorporating wonderful sustainable ingredients such as crisp garden salad, olives, grilled courgettes, aubergines and beetroot, and my favourite addition, grilled peaches or apricots, all washed down with a bottle of local ale. And to barbecue as ethically as possible try to source charcoal from sustainable sources, such as coppiced trees in locally managed woodland and forests.

SERVES » 4

For the marinated lamb
5 tablespoons olive oil
4 garlic cloves, finely chopped
small bunch of fresh oregano
freshly ground black pepper
4 x 160g slices lamb rump (also known
    as lamb chump chops)
For the yogurt sauce
a few sprigs of fresh oregano
75g full-fat natural yogurt or make
    your own (see page 199)
1 tablespoon runny honey
sea salt and freshly ground black pepper
For the salad
½ crunchy lettuce, like Cos,
    in bite-sized pieces
2 large tomatoes, quartered
¼ cucumber, deseeded and cubed
a small handful of de-stoned olives,
    roughly chopped
100g feta cheese, cubed
juice of 1 lemon
2 tablespoons olive oil

To serve
2 fresh peaches or 4 apricots
sea salt and freshly ground black pepper
4 large pitta breads
a few sprigs of oregano

The day before the barbecue, mix the marinade ingredients together in a bowl and dunk the lamb in it. Cover and refrigerate overnight.

To make the yogurt sauce, finely chop the oregano leaves, discarding the stalks, then mix with the yogurt and honey, and season to taste. Keep chilled. No more than 10 minutes before serving, put all the salad ingredients in a large bowl and toss.

When the barbecue is very hot, grill the peaches for 2 minutes and set aside. Add the lamb, discarding the marinade, and cook for 2–3 minutes on each side, seasoning well. Be careful not to overcook the lamb – you want the meat still pink and juicy but not bloody. Slice the meat and the peaches and keep them on a warm plate while you toast the pitta breads.

To serve, slice each pitta bread open, stuff with some of the salad, lamb and peaches, then spoon over some of the yogurt dressing and sprinkle with oregano leaves.

PLASTIC-FREE THAI FISH BURGER

Last summer we found ourselves with a whole day free to spend at the beach. The sun shone and despite a chilly north-easterly wind we barbecued fish burgers and were soon washing them down with ginger beer. Life is good when you combine great food, laughter and love. It was the perfect day. It was also the perfect burger.

What isn't so perfect is the amount of plastic waste that is polluting our oceans. The American Association for the Advancement of Science estimates it at eight million tonnes every year: equivalent to five full grocery bags for every foot of coastline in the world. The problem, though, isn't that all this garbage washes up on our beaches. If it did, it might be readily cleaned up, if we could just be concerned enough to deal with it. The real problem is that it stays in the water for a long time, breaking down into what are called 'micro plastics'. These are tiny fragments and fibres, which absorb pollutants such as oil, detergents, pesticides and methylmercury, and which then enter the food chain, because they are eaten by small marine organisms, which in turn are consumed by shrimp and the little fish on which larger fish may feed. This affects us because of a process called bioaccumulation: toxic substances can accumulate within a living creature to many times the background level of pollution, because they are absorbed at a much faster rate than they can be excreted or broken down, and at each step up the food chain, the concentration of the toxins increases. We are one of the creatures at the top of the marine food chain and so when we allow plastics to pollute the ocean, we are, without knowing the potential outcome, polluting one of our own food sources.

So what can we do? It's not enough to pick up the plastic litter we see on the beach or in the sea; we have to fundamentally change the way we think about plastic. More specifically, we need to limit the amount of plastic waste, whether it's a plastic bag we decide not to re-use or a drinks bottle that we don't recycle. Ultimately, it is only the collective actions of individuals that can prevent the situation from getting any worse.

SERVES » 4

For the burgers
500g skinless white fish fillets
200g skinless fresh tuna fillets
1 teaspoon fine sea salt
2 tablespoons sesame seeds
2 tablespoons soy sauce
1 tablespoon fish sauce
100g white breadcrumbs
1–2 red or green chillies, deseeded
    and finely chopped
3 garlic cloves, finely chopped
2 tablespoons capers in brine, drained,
    rinsed and chopped
small bunch of Thai basil, chopped
    (reserve ¼ for the mayonnaise)

To serve
4 slices of smoked bacon (optional)
4 sesame-topped burger buns, halved
4 lettuce leaves
2 medium tomatoes, sliced
80g mayonnaise, mixed with the
    reserved Thai basil

The trick to cooking these burgers is all in the preparation. Chop the white fish and tuna fillets very finely, ideally until almost minced. Sprinkle with the salt then refrigerate for a minimum of 2 hours (or up to 12). Drain any liquid from the fish then pat dry with kitchen paper, and transfer to a mixing bowl.

Add all the other burger ingredients to the bowl and mix evenly. Shape into four even-sized patties and put in the freezer for 20–30 minutes to firm up, on a tray lined with non-stick paper. If using, cook the bacon on a grill or barbecue until crisp. Set aside.

Toast the buns, then grill the burgers for 5–7 minutes on a medium heat until golden, turning just once as they are delicate. Serve with the bacon (if using), lettuce, tomatoes and mayonnaise on the toasted sesame seed buns.

MOTHER'S HOMEMADE DATE AND WALNUT GRANOLA BARS

These granola bars are great for a small child to make for Mother's Day with just a bit of supervision in the kitchen, as they don't require any complicated techniques. But the truth is that I am, more often, the person making them, to provide 'breakfast on the run' for my children; wrapped in greaseproof paper and ready to be thrust into the hand of a little one wailing 'I'm so late for school!' as she flies out the door, shoelaces undone, blazer flapping and school bag trailing. I know, however, that when she catches her breath on her way to the classroom, she'll be able to tuck into this chewy and filling bar, rich with seeds, nuts, oats and dates, and made with 'no added salt or sugar' puffed wheat, rather than running off to the sweet shop.

One fear we all have is that our baking might stick to the pan, even if it's had butter rubbed inside it first and a knife run round the tin after baking. Big business has responded by offering us all kinds of non-stick bakeware, liners and mats; but we might want to pause for thought. One popular non-stick coating for pans and cookware is PTFE: polytetrafluoroethylene. In itself, it is inert. But there are several reasons for concern. The first is that it can start to change above 200°C, and to deteriorate at 260°C – a temperature range that includes levels seen in domestic roasting and bread making, for example. It's also thought that scratching the non-stick surface with implements or when washing up damages the integrity of the remaining coating. But most of all, some of the chemicals used in making non-stick coating have acknowledged toxicity, and are 'persistent' in the environment and the human body: they don't pass through or degrade, but actually accumulate over the years. PFCs – perfluorinated compounds – are also potent contributors to greenhouse gases.

Cooking ethically and sustainably is not simply about what you cook but how you cook, and although manufacturers may reassure us that non-stick cookware is safe, I'm not sure that I buy that when the chemicals used to make the coatings are not. I'll stick to making my granola bars in an old-fashioned stainless steel pan.

MAKES ≈10 BARS

50g rolled oats

150g dates

75g unsalted butter

100g date syrup

90g puffed wheat

100g walnuts

35g pumpkin seeds

25g sunflower seeds

100g chocolate chips, (ideally 80 per
cent cocoa solids – optional)

Line a 24cm square x 6cm deep brownie tin with non-stick baking paper and preheat the oven to 180°C/160°C fan/gas 4. Spread the oats in a thin layer on a baking tray and toast them in the oven for 5 minutes, then remove and leave to cool. Chop the dates finely, then melt the butter in a saucepan with the dates and date syrup. Heat until warmed through, but do not boil.

Put the puffed wheat, walnuts and seeds in a large mixing bowl then pour in the date and butter mixture with the toasted oats and mix well. You can use your hands to mix them once the mixture is cool enough to handle, or a spoon or solid spatula. Mix in the chocolate chips, if using, then press the mixture firmly down into the lined tin. Bake for 20 minutes then leave to cool in the tin before cutting into bars. Store in an airtight container; they will keep for about a week.

LOCAL ROAST LEG OF LAMB with Moroccan spices

I grew up hand-rearing lambs every year. We'd have up to 40 at a time and they'd huddle under infrared lamps as we fed them their bottles of milk. Of course, they'd grow and we'd send them to the butchers just down the road in the horse trailer. I was always forlorn when the stables were empty. But what is even sadder, according to Compassion in World Farming, is that many live sheep and lambs are transported long distances before slaughter, not always given the rest, food or water they need, and suffer in overcrowded conditions. It is worse in summer when ventilation can be poor.

Please: buy lamb that hasn't been subjected to this treatment. Find a local butcher who sells lamb that has travelled the shortest distance from field to abbatoir, because this makes a big difference to the lambs' welfare. To take food activism one step further, ask there and at your local farmers' market for rare breed meat. For example, Llanwenog sheep are raised for meat rather than wool, and despite being relatively unusual, have some real advantages for small farmers. They are docile, prolific breeders – twin lambs are the norm – and because the lambs' birth size is quite small, the ewes have uncomplicated deliveries (some modern hybrids give bigger lambs, but the mothers can then have birth difficulties). The ewes give plenty of milk, so the youngsters grow quickly, and the breed can survive in marginal upland areas. Best of all, the meat is thought to have a superior flavour.

Your interest and concern in the lambs' welfare and in the type of meat you are buying, can make all the difference if the butcher knows it will influence the way you spend your money. Once again, what may seem like small steps can be the start of a different journey: and not just for you.

SERVES » 10

For the seasoning rub

1 head of garlic, halved: one half peeled and finely chopped, the other half unpeeled

1 small bunch rosemary, leaves only, finely chopped, plus extra sprigs

4 tablespoons olive oil

sea salt

3 tablespoons ras el hanout

2–2.5kg leg of lamb

250ml white wine or stock (optional)

Preheat the oven to 200°C/180°C fan/gas 6. Make the seasoning rub by mixing the chopped garlic, chopped rosemary, oil, salt and ras el hanout together.

Take a sharp knife and every 7.5cm or so, poke it about 5cm deep into the leg of lamb. Work the seasoning rub all over the meat, then place the leg in a roasting tin and push the rosemary sprigs into the cuts. Place the unpeeled half of the garlic under the lamb, so when it bakes it will flavour the gravy.

If you prefer pink roast lamb, cook it for just 1 hour 20 minutes. But my preference is to slow roast the meat, which produces a well-cooked but meltingly tender and delicious texture. To do this, pour the wine (or stock if you prefer) around the lamb, cover with foil, reduce the temperature to 120°C/100°C fan/gas ½ and roast for 7 hours.

BUTTERFLY EFFECT VICTORIA SPONGE CAKE

I cannot have a slice of cake without a cup of tea. So while this recipe is for a cake made with fair trade ingredients, I want to share a story about one of the tea pickers I met in the Nilgiri, or Blue Mountains, region of southern India.

I was watching a group of women pick the same tea that I drink at home. They were barefoot and brightly dressed, and I'd been told that they would sing as they worked. But they were incredibly shy. I suggested that we swap one song for another, and despite feeling self-conscious, I belted out an enthusiastic rendition of Shirley Bassey's 'Hey Big Spender'. It had the desired effect. The women, who had until this moment observed me with some suspicion fell about in a heap of giggles, and despite the language barrier, our laughter connected us. They relaxed and began to sing: a high-pitched trill, followed by an almost military marching-style chant, which one picker lead and the others repeated. It is a story of lost love, but it motivates the women as their picking matches the rhythm of the song.

Later on, when I'd sat through the official presentation about how fair trade helps with education and local projects, I spotted one of the ladies I'd met earlier that day. With the help of an interpreter, I asked how fair trade has helped her, but as she started to tell me, her voice broke, and in moments she was sobbing. She told me that her husband broke his legs and hips in an accident, and that when she was told, she thought her own life was over. If her husband died, she and her four young children were destined to live their lives as beggars, or worse, on the streets. They would be hungry, and they would suffer. She held my arm, and told me that I must thank the people who buy fair trade tea. She wanted them to know that because of them, her husband is alive. The fair trade premium helped to pay for his medical expenses and he recovered.

It's humbling to realise that a small decision you or I might make while shopping could affect another family in such an enormous way, but the truth is that you don't need to know their personal story to make the right decision. Fair trade makes a real difference to real people, and we can begin to change the world when we make a cake with fair trade ingredients, to share over a cup of fair trade tea.

SERVES »8

For the cake
250g caster sugar
250g self-raising flour
4 large eggs
250g unsalted butter, softened
2 tablespoons vanilla extract
For the filling
200g raspberry jam
300ml double cream
2 tablespoons icing sugar

I am going to go against convention with this cake, by using a 'one-step' method. Preheat the oven to 180°C/160°C fan/gas 4. Put the cake ingredients into the bowl of a stand mixer and beat slowly at first, increasing the speed until it runs on full for 2–3 minutes. Divide the mixture between two 23cm round cake tins and bake for 20–25 minutes, until firm to the touch. Cool on a wire rack.

Once the cakes are cool, spoon the jam onto the bottom layer. Whip the cream with half the icing sugar until it is thick but not overly stodgy. Spoon this carefully onto the jam and sandwich the layers of cake together. Finish off by dusting with the remaining icing sugar.

EARTH DAY OLIVE SHORTBREAD HEARTS

If I say 'Gaylord Nelson' to you, I'm not disclosing a secret about a great British naval hero; I am, instead, encouraging you to be inspired by an American who is perhaps not often remembered outside his own state of Wisconsin. Born in 1916, Nelson was a US Army captain in World War II, a white officer in charge of a unit of black soldiers, who protested at the way his men received second-class treatment because of their race. After serving as a state senator and governor, he was elected to the United States Senate for three consecutive terms, and as long ago as 1963, he persuaded President Kennedy to undertake a national tour talking about conservation issues. In 1969/70, he founded Earth Day, to promote the environmentalist cause. He went on to work with The Wilderness Society, to help protect unspoiled areas of natural beauty, and his best-known quotation is 'The economy is a wholly owned subsidiary of the environment, not the other way around'. He received America's highest civilian honour, the Presidential Medal of Freedom, and Bill Clinton said of him, 'As the father of Earth Day he is the grandfather of all that grew out of that event: the Environmental Protection Act, the Clean Air Act, the Safe Drinking Water Act'.

I've mentioned this because I think Senator Nelson demonstrated love and respect for the natural world and his fellow man. Love should be about cherishing what matters, not about buying an expensive gift that takes zero effort and contributes nothing, other than a little more pollution. By extension, loving means doing what is right. I believe that we need to cherish the Earth, so that our children and their children can live their lives to the full, and I believe that we can all make a difference: learning from the examples others have set, but making the right choices in our own lives.

Heart-shaped gifts are a classic way of expressing what we feel. With this recipe, you cannot only say 'I love you' to one other person, but also – by buying and using fair trade sugar, organic flour and olives, and farmers' market butter – send a quiet and personal message about caring for our world, and for the farmers and agricultural workers who have given us these wonderful things to enjoy. A message about protecting our planet, ethical food production, clean water, unpolluted air, healthy oceans, a childhood free from slavery and women's empowerment. An expression of love for us all.

MAKES ▸30 BISCUITS

100g caster sugar
250g unsalted butter, at room temperature
325g plain flour (I like to use rivet or another 'heritage' variety)
100g pitted black olives, quartered
2 tablespoons granulated sugar

Preheat the oven to 150°C/130°C fan/gas 2. Use an electric mixer, but only to cream the sugar and butter together until white and fluffy. Add the flour and combine, using a wooden spoon, possibly with your hands to finish. For the best texture, avoid kneading the dough more than is absolutely necessary. Add the olives and distribute them evenly, then roll the dough out to about 1cm thick and cut into heart shapes.

Place the shortbread shapes on a baking tray lined with non-stick baking paper, spaced slightly apart, and bake for 15–18 minutes. Be careful as the colour changes very quickly at the end of cooking, so be sure to keep a really close eye on them. Place on a wire rack to cool and sprinkle with the granulated sugar while still warm.

HELP THE HONEYBEE SPELT SOURDOUGH PANCAKES

Every year, I find some local honey for the children to give to their father, and rather like Pooh Bear, he stashes it away. I get him to share it on Sunday mornings though, because honey is perfect for drizzling on pancakes.

There's some evidence linking eating together as a family with children developing a healthier attitude towards food, as well as a stronger sense of wellbeing, better results at school and less antisocial behaviour. I know time is a problem if both parents have jobs or one parent isn't present, or you're simply working more hours to make ends meet, but I try to plan some meals where the whole family participates. Not just sitting down together, but with everyone playing an active part in making the food. No TV, mobile phones or social media, just conversation with the kids about their time at school, their friends, their plans. This recipe is my weekend standby.

Using honey also makes me think about the effort that local beekeepers put into looking after their hives. But our bees are in trouble; and if the bees are, then so are we. We need bees: it's estimated that they pollinate as much as 30 per cent of humanity's food crops, everything from figs, apples and avocados through to broccoli, onions and pumpkins and berries, nuts and spices. The sudden decline in their numbers seems to be caused by two factors: contamination of the pollen on which the bees feed by pesticides and fungicides; and then pests and parasites such as aethina, verroa and nosema attacking weakened bee populations. What we know is that if we lose our bees, we will lose a lot more than just honey: we will lose much of the world's food.

So here are five things you can do to help the honeybee. Let a corner of your garden go wild: weeds are often a food source for bees. Plant more bee-friendly flowers and herbs: the Royal Horticultural Society (RHS) publishes a list that you can find online. Don't use chemical sprays in your garden because they get carried back to the hive in pollen. Provide fresh water in a shallow container with some stones for bees to land on: bees need to drink. And find a local beekeeper who sells natural honey and buy two jars: one for you and one for a friend.

MAKES »15-16

250g unrefreshed 1-week-old
    sourdough starter (see page 41
    and page 192)
2 medium eggs
75g caster sugar
1 teaspoon mixed spice
½ teaspoon sea salt
175ml whole milk
200g spelt flour
1 teaspoon bicarbonate of soda
1½ teaspoons cream of tartar
2 tablespoons rapeseed oil
honey, soured cream and sliced
    bananas, to serve

Put the sourdough starter, eggs, sugar, mixed spice, salt and milk in a mixing bowl and whisk well.

Sift the flour, bicarbonate of soda and cream of tartar together into the sourdough mixture, stirring as you do so, just enough for the ingredients to be mixed to a consistent batter with no lumps.

Heat a little of the oil in a heavy-based frying pan over a medium heat for about 1 minute: not too hot. Add a ladleful of the batter to the centre of the pan and cook for about 1 minute.

Once the bottom is cooked to a light golden colour, flip the pancake over with a spatula and cook the other side. Watch what you are doing, as pancakes can burn really quickly. Transfer to a warm plate, covered with a clean tea towel, and continue to cook the remaining mixture in the same way, using the remaining oil to keep the pan lightly greased. Serve warm, drizzled with honey and soured cream, and topped with sliced bananas.

RECYCLE THE PEEL POLENTA CAKE

This is my 'plan ahead for Christmas' special, which is good at any time of year. I can't help associating oranges and spices with Christmas, and this golden, moist, gluten-free cake is a doddle to make. It tastes even better the next day... if you have the willpower to wait.

You can make the candied peel well in advance as it will keep for weeks. What you can also do is freeze the peel from unwaxed oranges as you use them (rather than buy four oranges just for this recipe), then thaw it for candying; and of course, you can make a bigger batch if you've saved up lots of peel. Just keep the ratio of 100g sugar added to every 100ml water reserved from the second, longer, boiling.

Home-cooked peel has an intense, bittersweet flavour and chewy texture, and is a fabulous addition to almost any cake. Or for a more indulgent treat, try dipping it halfway into melted dark chocolate, and let the chocolate set before eating. You can also make candied lemon peel for a lemon polenta cake in exactly the same way.

SERVES » 8

4 large unwaxed oranges

approx. 300g granulated sugar

250g unsalted butter, softened, plus
    extra for greasing

flour, for dusting

250g caster sugar

¼ teaspoon ground cardamom

250g ground almonds

125g fine polenta

2 teaspoons baking powder

4 medium eggs

zest of 2 unwaxed oranges

75g fine-cut orange marmalade

1 tablespoon water

Score each orange into eight segments, then carefully remove the peel and pith: cut the 5mm thick pieces into three or four bits. Put the peel in a pan and cover with 500ml cold water. Bring to the boil, simmer for 5 minutes, then drain and return to the pan. Add 500ml fresh cold water, bring to the boil and simmer for 30 minutes. Drain, but this time reserve and measure the water, adding 100g of sugar for each 100ml. There should be about 300ml, so 300g sugar. Put the water, sugar and peel back in the pan and simmer for 30 minutes until the sugar is dissolved and the peel is translucent and soft. Leave to cool. Lift the peel out of the syrup with a fork and arrange on a wire rack set over a baking tray. Leave to dry naturally over a couple of days, or put it in the oven on the lowest setting for 30 minutes. Store for up to eight weeks in an airtight container.

Preheat the oven to 180°C/160°C fan/gas 4. Line the base of a 23cm springform cake tin with nonstick baking paper, giving the sides a light buttering and dusting with flour.

Beat the butter and sugar together until fluffy.

Cut the peel into very small pieces and add to the bowl with the cardamom.

In a separate bowl, mix the ground almonds, polenta and baking powder together, and gradually add to the butter-sugar mixture, alternating with the eggs. Mix well, add the orange zest, then spoon the mixture into the tin and bake for about 25 minutes with a piece of baking paper over the top to stop it from catching. Reduce the temperature to 140°C/120°C fan/gas 2 and bake for a further 15–20 minutes.

When the cake is cooked, a skewer will come out clean and the edges will have shrunk away from the sides of the tin, but the cake will still have a slight wobble to it until it cools. Place it, in the tin, on a wire rack to cool.

Bring the marmalade and water to the boil for 30 seconds in a small pan to make a syrup. Prick the surface of the cake all over with a toothpick, then pour the warm syrup evenly over the top and leave to cool completely before removing the cake from the tin to serve.

HOMEMADE AND IMPROVER-FREE
SOUR CHERRY AND ALMOND STOLLEN

I was at a Christmas party last year, being chivvied and harassed by a rather determined host – think Mrs Doyle, from *Father Ted*. 'Merry Christmas! Glass of port? Slice of stollen? Go on!' What I heard was, 'Slice of mass-produced stollen packed with sodium stearoyl-2-lactylate, mono- and di-glycerides of fatty acids, acidity regulator, thickener, sorbitol syrup, glucose-fructose syrup, dextrose and palm oil... go on, go on, go on...'.

It saddens me that so many things get added in by factory bakeries, to taint a classic Christmas recipe. Simply put, volume-enhancers and emulsifiers have somehow become expected rather than the exception in many processed foods. These emulsifiers contain fats that, if subjected to high temperature processing such as baking, can create something called 'trans fats', associated with heart disease, strokes and diabetes. But because this trans fat gets created during processing, only the constituent parts need to be declared: not what is produced. We are assured that the risks associated with trans fats from emulsifiers are low, but we also know that we can bake without them.

I make this recipe with fair trade sour cherries, nuts and spices. Traditionally, stollen is brushed generously with melted butter and rolled in sugar as soon as it comes out of the oven, and as a result, it is a much better 'keeper' than other cakes, because it can retain more moisture. Occasionally, I find that it can get just a little bit too stodgy, so instead of using the melted butter method, I wrap a clean cotton tea towel around the cake as it cools, which keeps it moist without the extra fat.

SERVES » 8

150g unsalted butter
175g caster sugar
1 teaspoon bitter almond essence
zest of 1 unwaxed orange
1 teaspoon vanilla powder
1 tablespoon mixed spice
½ teaspoon fine sea salt
1 large free-range egg
150g double cream
150g unrefreshed 1–week-old
    sourdough starter (see page 41
    and page 192)
300g self-raising flour
100g ground almonds
175g sour cherries
icing sugar, to dust and to serve
200g marzipan
75g chopped or flaked almonds

Preheat the oven to 180°C/160°C fan/gas 4. Put the butter, sugar, bitter almond essence, orange zest, vanilla, mixed spice and salt into a large bowl and beat until smooth, then mix in the egg, cream and sourdough starter. Add the flour and ground almonds and work gently until the mixture forms a soft, slightly sticky dough. Stir in the cherries.

Dust the work surface with icing sugar and pat the dough out onto it, into an oval shape about 25cm x 15cm. Roll the marzipan into a 'rope' about 20cm long, and place it along the centre of the dough. Fold the dough in half over the marzipan, sealing the edges where they meet, and place it sealed-side down onto a baking tray lined with non-stick baking parchment. Brush the top of the stollen lightly with cold water and sprinkle with flaked almonds.

Bake for 1 hour 5 minutes, until golden. It is important not to over-bake. The almonds should be lightly toasted, and if you press with your finger, there will still be a slight 'give' in the dough. Test by inserting a skewer – it should come out clean. Remove from the oven, leave the stollen on the tray and while it is still slightly warm, wrap it in a clean tea towel. This keeps it moist as it cools.

The sourdough flavour develops over time, so once your stollen is completely cool, wrap it in greaseproof paper and then again in a fresh cotton tea towel, and leave to mature for 24 hours. Dredge with icing sugar and serve.

UNEXPECTED GUESTS

VEGAN-FRIENDLY BLACK BEAN AND MINT DIP

The most ethical and sustainable way to eat is to have a diet loaded with locally grown and seasonal vegetables. Now, I don't have the discipline and dedication to commit to a diet without meat, eggs or dairy, and find myself dipping in and out of ways and styles of eating. As a teenager I tried to be vegan, but failed. When I got over the initial guilt, I realised that what I could do was choose to eat vegan-friendly food occasionally. Today, when I cook my family a vegan meal no one actually misses animal products.

This recipe makes something very much like hummus, but instead of using chickpeas – the word hummus means 'chickpea' in Arabic — I use dried broad beans (sometimes labelled fava beans) or black beans. It's easy to make, stores for up to three days in the fridge and has many uses. It is superb spread on toasted sourdough bread, makes an excellent sandwich filler, and is a treat on a warm jacket potato. If you are in a hurry you can make this using canned beans, rinsed and drained: you then don't have to soak and boil the beans; just start the recipe at the point where they go into the food processor with the other ingredients.

SERVES » 4–6

200g dried black beans or broad beans
1 teaspoon bicarbonate of soda
5 tablespoons tahini
juice of 1 lemon
2 garlic cloves, crushed
4 tablespoons finely chopped fresh mint, plus extra to garnish
sea salt
extra virgin olive oil and sliced red chilli, to serve

The day before you cook, cover the dried beans with twice their volume of cold water. Stir in the bicarbonate of soda and leave to soak for 24 hours.

The following day, drain the beans, rinse well under cold running water and tip them into a large pan. Cover with fresh cold water, bring to the boil, then reduce the heat and simmer gently until the beans are tender enough to squash easily – this can take between 1 and 4 hours, depending on how old the beans are. Do remember to keep the water topped up, as you don't want them to boil dry.

Leave the beans to cool in the water. Drain well and reserve a few tablespoons of the cooking liquid and a few of the beans as garnish.

Put the beans, tahini, lemon juice and garlic in a food processor and pulse to make a purée. Add the mint, a generous pinch of salt and just enough cooking liquid (or tap water, if you've used canned beans) to make a soft paste. The dip should hold its shape and not be too wet. Check the seasoning and add more lemon juice, garlic or salt, according to taste.

Scrape the purée into a bowl, and when you are ready to serve, drizzle it with some olive oil and garnish with the reserved beans, more mint leaves and some sliced red chilli.

DON'T WASTE ME BECAUSE I'M RIPE GUACAMOLE

At home, if you are lucky, you might buy an avocado at the perfect point of ripeness on the exact day you want to eat it. If it is ready, you can tell by holding the pear in one hand and pressing it gently with your thumb. If it yields, then it is ripe. But often, you have to buy an avocado a little on the hard side and put it in the fruit bowl to ripen. If you leave it too long and miss that day when it is ripe yet still firm, you go past that perfect moment. The ideal texture is lost and the thumb test would almost dent the flesh.

When you consider what has gone into providing you with your avocado – the energy to make fertiliser to feed the tree, the hands that picked and packed it – and the carbon-cost of transporting it thousands of miles, it is beyond exasperating if it ends up in the bin. It is worth taking a moment to check if it really has gone too far to be eaten or if you have caught it at the very moment it will make perfect guacamole.

SERVES » 4

3 ripe avocados
½ teaspoon fine sea salt
juice of 1 fresh lime or small lemon
1 spring onion, thinly sliced
small bunch of fresh coriander, leaves
   finely chopped
freshly ground black pepper
pinch of smoked paprika
1 red chilli, stems and seeds removed,
   minced, plus extra to garnish
1 ripe tomato, seeds and pulp removed,
   chopped

Halve the avocados, peel them and remove the stones. Trim off any brown bits and, using a fork, roughly mash the flesh in a bowl, but be careful not to overdo it: there is joy in the chunks. Sprinkle with the salt and lime or lemon juice. The acid in the juice delays the oxidisation of the avocado, which would otherwise turn it an unappetising dark colour. Add the spring onion and coriander (reserving a few leaves to serve), a few twists of black pepper, the smoked paprika and chilli. Stir.

Refrigerate until needed. Remove from the fridge about 30 minutes before serving as this improves the flavour. When you're ready, stir in the tomato (leaving that step until now prevents the tomato softening in the lemon juice and keeps the texture firmer). Delicious served with warm sourdough flatbread (page 48).

NATURAL BAKED CHEESE

I picked up a lovely Normandy Camembert last week. I was about to add it to my shopping trolley when I stopped myself and put it back. Old habits die hard though, and I'll always have a fondness for French cheese. When I was growing up, it seemed difficult to find British cheeses beyond Cheddar, a rather rubbery Red Leicester and Stilton, while the French were the masters of the (cheesy) universe. But today, British cheesemaking has progressed to such an extent that even our neighbours across the Channel have noticed.

One of my favourite 'new' British cheeses is Tunworth, which is made in Hampshire, by a small family-run business that pays a fair price for the milk they buy from their local dairy farmers. No peculiar additives, just milk with their own cheese-making culture (rather like yogurt) and a little rennet mixed in, to encourage the curds to begin to set, naturally, over the following hours. Then the curds are cut into cubes and placed into round moulds, and left overnight for the whey to drain off, before being lightly salted and taken to the ripening room, where the cheese starts to develop its characteristic slightly wrinkly white rind. Finally, the cheese will spend several weeks in the maturing room, before being taken to market or sent to the purchaser.

Cheese is often overlooked as a sustainable food. It turns milk – a very perishable product – into something with a much longer shelf life, preserving its nutritional value for the consumer and its economic value for the dairy farmer. The simple stages of production are natural methods of preservation (dampness would hasten decomposition, but draining the whey prevents that, and then the carefully controlled addition of salt prevents excess acidity and, along with the development of a natural rind, halts any unhelpful bacterial growth). Like any agricultural process, it is open to industrialisation, and I find 'processed' cheese to be one of the most depressing products in the supermarket. But when you want something truly delicious to share, a baked cheese like Tunworth is just the ticket.

SERVES ▸ 4

1 whole 250g Tunworth or another
   Camembert-style cheese
1 garlic clove, very finely sliced
sprig of fresh rosemary, leaves only
olive or rapeseed oil

Preheat the oven to 180°C/160°C fan/gas 4. Remove the cheese from its box, discarding the lid and the waxy wrapping paper. Put a piece of baking parchment just big enough to come slightly above the sides into the base of the box, and put the cheese back in its place. Gently make diagonal cuts into the top layer of rind, then poke the garlic slivers and rosemary leaves into the holes with your fingers, or with the help of a table knife. Drizzle with oil then bake for 15–20 minutes, or until melted and unctuous in the middle.

I love to serve this drizzled with a teaspoon of dark runny honey. In late summer, I simply add a plate of sliced ripe figs, and for the rest of the year I serve it with breadsticks and fresh dates.

LAST-MINUTE VEGETABLE TEMPURA

Whenever guests drop by, I want them to stay longer. The best way to do this is by feeding them: food makes everyone feel welcome. However, I don't keep a fully-stocked larder on the off-chance that people will call in. But if I look in the fridge, I'll almost always have some spare fresh vegetables. Sometimes, like socks not quite matching and never the right assortment for farmhouse soup: half an aubergine, a single carrot, some button mushrooms and tomorrow's cauliflower. Individually, not up to much, but chopped, seasoned and deep-fried they become fluffy and crisp tempura, a Japanese delicacy. And suddenly you have a sophisticated, inexpensive meal. The last time I made this, I used courgettes, aubergine, fennel, celery and some par-boiled potato and sweet potato; it's easy to adapt to whatever you have to hand.

400g assorted vegetables

fine sea salt and freshly ground black
    pepper or some ground spices

For the dipping sauce

20ml soy sauce

30ml rice wine

20ml runny honey

¼ red chilli, deseeded and very finely
    chopped

2.5–5cm piece of fresh root ginger,
    peeled, and the juice squeezed

For frying

approx. 750ml sunflower oil

100g plain flour

20g cornflour

1 teaspoon Chinese five spice powder

5g teaspoon fine sea salt

5g baking powder

225ml ice-cold sparkling mineral water

3 large ice cubes

Cut the vegetables into pieces roughly 1cm thick, and ideally about 8–9cm long and 4–5cm wide. If you are using potato or sweet potato, par-boil and thoroughly drain them; otherwise, raw is best. Sprinkle with fine sea salt to draw out some of the moisture, and leave for 1 hour. Pat dry with a clean tea towel, then season with a grinding of black pepper, or spices of your choice. Prepare the dipping sauce by putting all the ingredients into a small bowl and stirring well.

Heat the oil in a large work or deep fryer until it reaches 190°C.

As it heats, make the batter by mixing all the dry ingredients together in a large bowl, then whisking in the ice-cold water and adding the ice cubes. Mix quickly, using a whisk: a few lumps do not matter but do not overbeat, as it will make a chewy rather than light and crispy batter. Do not dilly-dally: dip the vegetables into the batter one piece at a time, then drop them carefully into the hot oil, taking care not to splash yourself. Cook for a minute or so, until a light golden colour. Remove with clean chopsticks or a slotted spoon and place on kitchen paper to remove any excess oil. The secret to successful tempura is having everything ready, not delaying at any stage, and not overfilling the pan.

Serve immediately with the dipping sauce on the side. Good with some plain steamed sticky rice, or over thin soba (buckwheat) noodles.

FOOD SECURITY FISH PÂTÉ

In my early twenties, I went out on a small fishing boat off the coast of West Africa with a crew of eleven local fishermen. It was an incredible experience and one that showed me just how hard they worked to make their living. As night-time fell, the nets were cast and then pulled through the water. Not long after, the engines were cut. As the nets were winched up and the catch hauled on deck, they seemed full of fish. Silver, shining, their scales catching the light of the moon as they danced their last across the bottom of the boat.

The men worked fast, sorting what was to be kept from what was not, throwing the unwanted part of the catch back into the water, still alive. I remember their respect for the ocean, their tight-knit community and that they were able to feed their families in harmony with the environment. It was a far cry from the global fishing industry, which is notorious for environmental abuses and a short-term approach. Greenpeace has reported on European supertrawlers, which have moved into the fishing grounds off Mauretania; there legitimately, by agreement with that country's government, but fishing on a scale that is hard to comprehend. They calculate that one of these giant ships can catch in one day what 50–60 traditional West African fishing boats catch in a year. To me, this smacks of stealing the livelihood of local fishing communities and exporting the overfishing, which has so badly damaged European fish stocks.

I think we can make a difference to the lives of people like those African fishermen if we think about two small words when we buy fish: sustainably sourced. In some cases it means you are not just looking after the ecosystem of the ocean, but also choosing not to endanger the food security of traditional communities, and showing some respect for their way of life.

Though this pâté is excellent made with sustainable canned tuna or mackerel, I prefer to make it with British freshwater trout, which also avoids food miles. Most trout is farmed, and buying organic is the best choice, as welfare is generally higher, fish stocking densities are lower and the feed used is sourced sustainably; but you could even catch the fish yourself! It's a simple dish that can be made in minutes, leaving you to get on with chatting to your guests, especially if you have some sourdough bread in the freezer ready to toast. If you are baking your own whole fish, then 1kg uncooked will give you about 500g flesh, once the bones and skin are discarded.

SERVES » 4–6

500g cooked trout fillets, skinned
   and boned
juice of 2 small lemons
300g full-fat soft cheese
pinch of sea salt
freshly ground black or white pepper
a handful of finely chopped fennel leaves
   or dill

Put the trout fillets into a bowl and break them up with a fork. Using your fingers, check through the fish to ensure there are no stray bones. Add the lemon juice and cheese then mix well. Season with salt and black or white pepper, stir in the herbs and press quite firmly into a serving dish. It's ready to serve.

SUPPORT YOUR LOCAL MILLER
SOURDOUGH PAPPARDELLE with herb butter

It may seem a little crazy to make homemade pasta when a friend drops in, but before you dismiss this as impractical, let me say this: it is fun, it doesn't take long and making pasta is always easier with two sets of hands. It is also wonderfully simple food that can be enjoyed for what it is – simple, rustic and inexpensive.

I try to support small independent millers, and if you look online you might be surprised to find one near where you live. What I've chosen to use here is an organic coarse semolina flour milled from English wheat at an historic windmill in Cambridgeshire: perfect for this recipe.

SERVES » 4

For the dough
250g semolina flour, plus extra
    for dusting
5g fine sea salt
5 egg yolks
225g unrefreshed 1-week-old
    sourdough starter (see page 41
    and page 192)
oil, for greasing
For the herb butter
a handful of very finely chopped fresh
    herbs, such as oregano, basil, chives,
    coriander or parsley.
3–4 tablespoons unsalted butter,
    slightly softened
sea salt and freshly ground black pepper
a chunk of fresh Parmesan cheese

Mix the semolina flour with the salt then tip it into a pile onto a clean, smooth work surface. Make a well in the middle of the flour then add the egg yolks and starter. Work the flour into the wet ingredients, first with a wooden spoon and then with your hand, to make a firm dough. Depending on the thickness of your starter, you may need to add a little extra flour or an extra yolk, but before making any adjustments really bring this mixture together tightly with your hands, as it is easy to misjudge.

Knead the dough until it is smooth, then transfer it to an oiled bowl. Cover with a clean, damp cloth and leave it to rest for 20 minutes. This allows the gluten to relax, making the dough easier to roll out and handle again.

Meanwhile, make some herb butter. Put the herbs in a bowl, add the butter, salt and black pepper, and mash with a fork so that the herbs and seasoning are evenly distributed. You can make this in advance, and keep it in the fridge until you need to use it.

Once rested, either roll the dough out very thinly on a floured surface with a rolling pin and cut into long thick strips, or use a pasta maker and cut into 2cm wide ribbons or 'pappardelle'. Arrange into 12 separate 'nests', sit them on a tray generously dusted with semolina, and set aside somewhere cool until you're ready to cook them.

Cook the pasta in salted boiling water for just 2 minutes – much less than you would dried pasta – then drain and serve with some of the herb butter tossed through and sprinkled with a generous scattering of Parmesan. I love to use generous curls of Parmesan cut with a vegetable peeler from a larger piece, which are just as chunky as the pappardelle.

SAVE MY BACON ORZO

Not so many years ago, the ex-husband of a friend had to pick something up from the field where my family were keeping pigs. He'd not behaved well towards his wife and we'd heard that he treated his car with more care than he'd shown her. He arrived in his new BMW and, yes, the car was clearly his pride and joy.

The pigs were enormous. They were Large White crosses, as long as the car was wide. Pigs are naturally inquisitive and sociable animals and knew my brother would have something good to eat, so they wandered over to check out what was going on. A few moments later there was a shriek; because what does a truly free-thinking and free-range pig do when given the chance? Seeing a door left open, one sow had climbed onto the back seat and made herself very comfortable. Like the Queen of Sheba, lying full length across the butter-soft cream leather, no amount of shouting or kicking, swearing or prodding was going shift her from this comfortable situation. It was a true James Herriot moment. My brother told us later that he was absolutely certain that the sow knew exactly what she was doing. They did eventfully shift her, but not before the seats in the car were well and truly covered in mud and pig shit, and our visitor had worked himself up into in a terrible temper. We felt there was a certain poetic justice, and I have to admit we found it very funny!

Pigs are not without charm, personality and intelligence. They are curious, can be trained to seek out truffles and one American study found that they could even be taught to play simple video games, so what is not so funny is the way in which pigs are factory farmed. They are confined in metal cages, on concrete floors, denied daylight and forced to behave in a way that is completely against their instincts. It is beyond cruel to treat any creature this way and I don't believe we have to treat an animal badly just because we are going to eat it. In fact, we should remember that it will die to feed us, and treat it kindly and with some respect.

This recipe doesn't need much bacon. Really good, well-cured bacon tastes delicious and has so much flavour that a small amount goes a long way.

SERVES » 4–6

2 tablespoons olive oil
200g smoked bacon lardons
1 large onion, finely chopped
3 garlic cloves, sliced
1 bay leaf
3 sprigs of lemon thyme
50g unsalted butter
400g orzo
800ml hot chicken stock
200g peas
½ lemon, Parmesan-style cheese
   and paprika, to serve

Heat the oil in a large saucepan, fry the lardons until crisp then lift them out with a slotted spoon onto a plate. Reduce the heat, add the onion and garlic, and cook until soft and translucent. Then add the bay leaf, lemon thyme, butter and orzo. Stir for 1 minute then gradually add about three quarters of the chicken stock, one ladle at a time, stirring constantly. Add the peas, lardons and remaining stock, stir well and cover with the lid. Reduce the heat and simmer for 5 minutes.

Remove from the heat and leave for 3 minutes with the lid on. Check that the stock has all been absorbed. If not, leave for a few minutes more. Fluff with a fork, squeeze the juice from the lemon into the pan and serve with curls of Parmesan-style cheese and a dusting of paprika.

EAT LESS MEAT STIR-FRY

OK, we've all stepped to the left or right to avoid the crazy man with mad hair and a placard, ringing a bell and shouting at us that the end of the world is nigh. But he may not be quite as crazy as you think.

The UN's Intergovernmental Panel on Climate Change draws on the work of thousands of experts around the world and it has told us quite bluntly that unless carbon emissions are cut sharply and rapidly, climate change is set to inflict 'severe, widespread and irreversible impacts' on both the environment and human populations. Their report also found that dietary change can 'substantially lower' emissions and yet there is, so far, no UN plan for doing this. Buried in all the warnings were two positive messages however: that 'it is economically affordable' to reduce carbon emissions that will ultimately have to fall to zero, and that 'global poverty can only be reduced by stopping global warming'.

One of the most powerful actions that we can take is to reduce our meat and dairy consumption significantly. The UN Food and Agriculture Organization, in a 2013 report, told us that almost 15 per cent of 'anthropogenic' (caused by human activity) greenhouse gas emissions come from the livestock industry; by animal, mostly relating to beef and milk production and by sector, from feed manufacturing and processing, and the methane gas generated from animals' digestive systems.

So here I am writing a recipe to use less meat in a stir-fry. I know that's just the smallest step, but to paraphrase the philosopher Lao-Tzu, that is the only way to start 'a journey of a thousand miles'. I know that we have the means to limit climate change and that inaction is quite literally going to cost us the earth, so we must not be afraid to start with modest choices and decisions.

This recipe uses just 50g meat per person, but is filled with vegetables to ensure that no one at the table goes hungry, and it can be cooked in just a few minutes for family or friends.

SERVES » 4

3–4 tablespoons vegetable oil

200g beef steak, very thinly sliced

150g mushrooms, thinly sliced

1 large red pepper, thinly sliced

2 courgettes, cut into ribbons

2 red or green chillies, deseeded
   and chopped

2 garlic cloves, chopped

6 large spring onions, finely chopped

150g bean sprouts, washed

3–4 tablespoons soy sauce

juice of 1 lime

5–7.5cm piece of fresh root ginger,
   peeled, grated and the juice squeezed

sesame oil

a handful of fresh coriander

1 tablespoon toasted sesame seeds

Put a wok over a high heat, add the vegetable oil and bring it just to the point of smoking. Add the beef and mushrooms, a handful at a time, giving them time to get hot before adding more. Keep the heat high all the time and the wok moving with one hand, and stir with the other. Add the red pepper, courgettes and three quarters of the chillies, and then the garlic and spring onions, and cook for a further 2 minutes.

Add the bean sprouts, soy sauce, lime juice, ginger juice and a drizzle of sesame oil. Keep stirring over a high heat for a further minute then serve immediately with a generous scattering of coriander, sesame seeds and the remaining chillies.

Excellent served with plain boiled noodles or steamed rice.

PRESERVATIVE-FREE SOURDOUGH BLUEBERRY MUFFIN CAKE

If you pick up a plastic-wrapped, commercially produced muffin you can expect to see preservatives, emulsifiers and stabilisers in the ingredients. Yet muffins are so easy and quick to make at home with none of these additives that buying them seems almost like lunacy to me. But sometimes I want a cake I can slice, rather than a muffin, and then I make this large muffin cake.

This cake is the opposite of the slowly fermented sourdough loaves I love to make, because I can have it in the oven in under ten minutes and on the table ready to eat not long after that. Very quick to make and delicious warm from the oven: perfect for when you're waiting for your sourdough loaf.

I also like this recipe because it helps me avoid throwing sourdough starter away, especially as the bacteria has done an amazing job of transforming the flour into something more digestible with an intense and complex sour flavour. But if you don't have any sourdough on the go, simply leave it out and the recipe will still work just fine. You can also use raspberries, pears, plums or rhubarb in the cake instead of blueberries if you like.

MAKES »12 portions of cake
(or 12 muffins)

butter, for greasing
150g unrefreshed 1-week-old
    sourdough starter (see page 41 and
    page 192)
pinch of salt
50ml rapeseed oil
150g caster sugar
220ml whole milk
1 medium egg
230g self-raising flour
220g blueberries
For the topping
75g granulated sugar
75g ground almonds
75g unsalted butter, softened
50g flaked almonds

Preheat the oven to 180°C/160°C fan/gas 4 and lightly butter a 24cm square, 6cm deep tin.

Measure the sourdough starter, salt, oil, caster sugar and milk into a mixing bowl, add the egg and whisk thoroughly, then fold in the flour. In a separate bowl, rub the granulated sugar, ground almonds and butter for the topping together, until they resemble breadcrumbs.

Spoon the cake mixture into the tin (or divide it between a dozen muffin cases sitting in the pockets of a 12-hole muffin tray). Smooth the mixture lightly on top and dot with the blueberries.

Sprinkle with the topping mixture, scatter with the flaked almonds and bake for 18–20 minutes or until a skewer inserted into the middle comes out clean.

FEEDING CHILDREN

SUSTAINABLE MINI FISH PIES

There is a temptation when you are tired at the end of a long day to cave in and buy a ready meal. The supermarkets specialise in making the picture on the packaging look as homemade as possible to alleviate your guilt, but the truth is that no matter how lovely the photo is, a fish pie is something that always tastes better when you make it yourself. These mini fish pies can be frozen to use later and are perfect for fuss-free suppers that ethically sustain both your children and our cod and haddock stocks. I cook a double batch of the recipe and freeze half.

Cod is a firm favourite with children as its firm meaty texture is easy to eat, but like many species of fish it has at times been fished to the edge of extinction. In the colder waters to the north of Iceland it takes seven years for even half the juveniles to attain sexual maturity, but only five years in the warmer waters to the south. So to keep on enjoying cod, it is important to fish it sustainably. Look for the Marine Stewardship Council label when you buy.

MAKES » 8 mini fish pies
(or 4 adult-sized main dishes)

750g cod
250g haddock
600ml whole milk, plus extra if necessary
3 bay leaves
4–5 sprigs of lemon thyme
75g unsalted butter
75g plain flour
30ml rapeseed oil
2 leeks, washed and thinly sliced
salt and freshly ground pepper, to taste
a handful of fresh chopped parsley
25g grated Parmesan cheese
½ teaspoon freshly grated nutmeg
750g mashed potatoes
125g sourdough breadcrumbs mixed
    with an extra 25g grated Parmesan
    cheese

Check the fish for any stray bones, then place it in a large shallow pan with the milk, bay leaves and thyme. Bring almost to the boil then reduce the heat and simmer for just 5 minutes, so the fish is barely cooked.

Remove the pan from the heat then drain and lift out the fish pieces onto a plate, and remove any skin. Strain the milk and measure it; you want about 500ml, so top it up if necessary. Discard the herbs.

Wash the pan, clean off any milk residue stuck to the inside then return it to the stove and melt the butter in it over a moderate heat. Add the flour, stir well, then reduce the heat and cook gently for about 2 minutes, stirring constantly. Gradually beat in the milk from the fish a little at a time to make the sauce, still stirring constantly until smooth. Do not rush. Simmer for 8–10 minutes, stirring frequently.

Meanwhile, in a separate large, heavy saucepan, cook the leeks in the oil until they are soft. Cover the pan but don't brown them –

they just need to be translucent. Once cooked, stir the leeks into the sauce. Season with salt and black pepper, and beat in the parsley and Parmesan.

Flake the fish into chunks and divide it between eight small or four larger individual ovenproof (and freezer-proof) dishes, adding enough sauce to fill them about two thirds of the way up the sides. Add the nutmeg to the mashed potatoes and mix it in well, then fill each dish to the top with the mash, and last of all, a scattering of sourdough breadcrumbs. You can freeze the pies at this point. Cover the tops with greaseproof paper then wrap in foil before freezing. Leave to thaw in the refrigerator before baking.

When you are ready to bake, preheat the oven to 170°C/150°C fan/gas 3. Remove any wrapping from the pies and bake for 35–45 minutes or until crisp and golden on top, with the filling piping hot and bubbling.

COMPASSIONATE CHICKEN NUGGETS

The food that I feed my family and loved ones reflects my feelings for them. I know how fussy children can be, and also I know the temptation of cheap frozen processed food, designed to appeal to children. But even at a time when we're all challenged financially I try to pause and consider the true cost of that food.

Take cheap chicken nuggets, for example. To achieve that bargain price, the welfare of the animal probably won't have been the highest concern. By breeding chickens that grow to slaughter weight in less than six weeks – half the time it would have taken thirty years ago – companies save on time, space and labour. So we twist nature to satisfy our clamouring for cheap processed food. Meat gets mechanically recovered – scraped, processed, sieved and reformed, if that sounds better to you – and the process means that although bone and beak may be detected and removed, there is an increased risk of microbial growth because the finely pulped 'meat' has a greater surface area.

The answer is to make your own. That way you can choose the chicken that suits you and prepare it in a way that will give you confidence. Children love soft chicken in a crunchy coating. Come to think about it, so do grown-ups, especially when there's a touch of garam masala in the coating. One hundred per cent breast meat chicken nuggets are the perfect alternative to the reconstituted who-knows-what's-in-them frozen variety, and are both compassionate and delicious.

SERVES » 3

3 chicken breasts, weighing approx.
    400g
250ml whey, left over from draining
    mozzarella or yogurt (or use
    buttermilk)
200g breadcrumbs, ideally
    sourdough ones
salt and freshly ground black pepper
1 teaspoon garam masala
150ml rapeseed oil
For the garlic dip
100g full-fat crème fraîche
1 garlic clove, finely chopped
¼ teaspoon sea salt
2 sprigs of parsley, chopped

The day before cooking, prepare the chicken (you can marinate it for just a few hours if you are short of time). Put one chicken breast between two sheets of greaseproof paper, laying it as flat as possible. If it's particularly large, you may need to cut through the thickest part using a sharp knife and fold it open to make it flatter.

Lay a clean tea towel on top of the greaseproof paper. Hold the chicken in place with one hand, then lightly bash it with a rolling pin until it is about 1–1.5cm thick. Repeat with the other chicken breasts (make sure to wash the tea towel afterwards to avoid any contamination).

Take each chicken breast and cut it into 6–8 pieces, put them into a bowl, add the whey, cover and leave in the fridge to marinate for 24 hours.

When you are ready to cook the chicken, mix the breadcrumbs, salt, black pepper and garam masala together in a wide, shallow dish. Shake the excess buttermilk off the chicken pieces and press them into the breadcrumbs until evenly coated.

To make the garlic dip, mix all the ingredients together in a small bowl.

Heat the oil in a large, heavy pan and gently add some of the chicken pieces; reduce the heat to low and cook for about 3 minutes on each side until golden. Take care not to overload the pan and turn the pieces once. Transfer onto kitchen paper once cooked to blot off any excess oil and keep warm on a tray in a warm oven while you cook the remaining chicken. Serve with the garlic dip on the side.

STEWARDSHIP FISH GOUJONS

We are overfishing the seas. Modern fishing is an industrial operation: ships use technologically advanced fish-detecting sonar to find a school of fish with almost military precision. Trawlers have been replaced by huge factory ships, with on-board processing, freezing and packing facilities, even a fishmeal processing plant. The largest of these vessels can process 350 tonnes of fish a day, and can store 7,000 tonnes of fully processed catch. To put that into perspective: it's the equivalent of a freezer holding 35 million 200g portions of filleted fish, in one gigantic ship, on one fishing expedition.

It's little surprise then that after just a few decades of industrial sea fishing the result is that many species are under threat. So how do we know what to buy?

The Marine Stewardship Council sets standards for sustainable fishing and seafood traceability, and provides a list of sustainable species and fisheries. But it's even easier than that: you can look for its blue 'Certified Sustainable Seafood' label on packaging and menus, even in the windows of fish and chip shops that have switched to sustainable sources of fish, making it easier to choose. But it's still essential that we check, and buy fish that aren't endangered. The bottom line is that if we keep eating fish that are under threat, then by the time our children grow up, some species may no longer even be on the MSC list at all: we will have eaten them into extinction.

SERVES » 4

For the goujons
2 garlic cloves, peeled
zest of 1 large lemon
400g (about 6 slices) sourdough bread
30ml olive oil, plus extra for greasing
4 sprigs of fresh tarragon
½ teaspoon sea salt
freshly ground black pepper
3 heaped tablespoons plain flour
2 large eggs
540g white fish fillets, skinned and
    deboned, cut into 2.5cm strips
rapeseed oil, for frying
lettuce leaves, to serve
For the tartare sauce
100g homemade mayonnaise
    (page 210)
30g pickled capers, rinsed, patted
    dry and chopped
30g pickled gherkins, finely chopped
a handful of chopped parsley
juice of ½ large lemon
1 shallot, finely chopped
sea salt and freshly ground black pepper

Put the garlic, lemon zest and bread into a food processor. Add the olive oil, tarragon, salt and black pepper, then whizz until the mixture is reduced to very fine breadcrumbs. Tip out into a shallow dish.

Spoon the flour onto a plate. Crack the eggs into a bowl and beat with a fork. Dip the fish into the flour until both sides are completely coated, then dip into the egg and lastly into the flavoured breadcrumbs. If the crumbs are not sticking, then you can press the fish into them gently to get them to stay on – you really want the fish to be completely coated.

You can either bake or fry the goujons. To bake, preheat the oven to 240°C/220°C fan/gas 9, place the fish on a baking tray brushed with 1 tablespoon of olive oil and cook for 15 minutes. If frying, put a frying pan over a medium heat, fill no more than one third deep with rapeseed oil and cook the fish for 4 minutes on each side – the pieces should be golden and crisp.

To make the tartare sauce, stir all the ingredients together in a small bowl.

Serve the goujons wrapped in lettuce leaves, with a little tartare sauce.

HOMEMADE AND HERITAGE OVEN-BAKED CHIPS

I have to admit that it is tempting to grab a bag of oven-ready chips from the freezer cabinet. While there are lots of different cuts and styles of chips on sale in the supermarket – crinkle cut, chunky, microwavable, even curly ones – we sadly rely on just nine retail chains who control 95 per cent of the grocery market to supply them. These companies demand very specific sizes and types of potato from the processors and wholesalers. It is a very restrictive place to be, for the farmers at the very bottom of the chain, especially if their potatoes fail to meet the grade. Rejected potatoes can often only be sold cheaply as animal feed and this puts farmers in a desperate financial situation.

The inequalities of the market mean that farmers don't have much choice where they sell their potatoes, or how much they get for them, and likewise, we as consumers miss out on variety, taste and flavour in the name of uniformity and ease of production. But are we getting great chips? I don't think so. Ready-made chips are predictable, homogenous, bland. There are over 4,000 varieties of potatoes out there, and supermarkets give us a choice of maybe five or six.

You can really support diversity and fairer trading while vamping up your chips by buying more unusual potato varieties directly from the farmers. Or try growing some heritage potatoes yourself. Some of these varieties have almost been lost completely as they are not grown commercially. Potatoes don't have to be white; there are purple, blue and red potatoes, with the most marvellous textures and flavour.

I bake my chips as this means you can use any potato variety, without worrying about whether it will hold up to frying. This also means I can flavour the chips: I love using sea salt and black pepper, but garlic and rosemary, or even ground spices such as cumin or fennel, work really well. Add a couple of tablespoons of any of these combinations for every four large potatoes in with the basic seasoning and you will have the most personalised and delicious chips.

1–2 large potatoes, per person
2–3 tablespoons olive or rapeseed oil, per potato
salt and freshly ground black pepper

I don't peel the potatoes if the skin is good. Simply chop them into chip shapes. Bear in mind that the bigger they are, the longer they will take to bake.

Put the potatoes in a large pan of salted cold water and bring them to the boil, then drain them in a colander and tip them into a large bowl. Drizzle them with a generous amount of oil.

Preheat the oven to 200°C/180°C fan/gas 6. Meanwhile, leave the potatoes for 5–10 minutes to cool, then season with salt and black pepper.

Mix with either a couple of wooden spoons or your hands. Spread the potatoes onto baking trays, but leave space between them for the heat to circulate. If you feel that they need a little more oil, drizzle some on. Bake for 20 minutes.

Remove from the oven and turn them with a pair of tongs, then return to the oven and cook for a further 10–15 minutes, depending on how thick you cut them. Cook until they are golden. Serve immediately, with a sprinkling of salt if you feel they need more.

DON'T DESTROY THE RAINFOREST DIGESTIVES

The humble digestive biscuit is one of the all-time classics, with crumbs that beg to be picked up and nibbled, a texture fit to dunk in milky tea, and rich with a nutty, sweet and almost buttery flavour. But would people still think they were quite so delightful if they knew the story about the palm oil used as the fat in many well-known brands?

Palm oil production is responsible for the destruction of tropical rainforests, particularly in south-east Asia and most notably in Indonesia and Malaysia. It's not just the loss of habitat for animals such as orang-utans, rhinos, elephants and tigers that makes palm oil unacceptable: indigenous peoples living in those rainforests lose their land and with it their way of life when the land is granted as a 'concession' to a plantation company. In May 2013, the World Wildlife Fund (WWF) even announced that using palm oil certified as 'sustainable' was no longer enough to be sure that companies were acting responsibly, adding that the criteria being applied did not require producers to account for greenhouse gas emissions or clearance of carbon-rich peatland.

It also saddens me that in 2014, one biscuit manufacturer that had previously switched to using reduced saturated fat sunflower oil in its digestives then got press coverage about how it was 'listening to customers' and switched back to a 'classic' recipe using palm oil (top tip: I don't think palm oil was a 'classic' ingredient in British baking, and it was also admitted that the sunflower oil recipe was more expensive to produce).

So what can we do about it? Start by avoiding products that contain palm oil and check with the manufacturers what they mean by 'vegetable fats in varying proportions' in their food labelling. Better still, make your own biscuits with butter, the way they were made years ago. The biscuits made in this recipe taste so good that you just can't stop eating them, and now there really is no excuse to unwittingly contribute to the destruction of the rainforests while you sit and dunk a digestive biscuit in your tea.

MAKES » 25 BISCUITS

180g wholemeal flour, plus extra
  for dusting
200g medium oatmeal
½ teaspoon bicarbonate of soda
65g light muscovado sugar
½ teaspoon sea salt
170g unsalted butter, cold and diced
50g unrefreshed 1-week-old
  sourdough starter (optional –
  see page 41 and page 192)

The easiest way to make these biscuits is to put all the ingredients in a food processor and pulse a few times to combine until the mixture looks damp and comes together in a rough dough. If you don't have a food processor, simply combine the flour with the other dry ingredients in a bowl before rubbing in the butter (and sourdough starter, if using) with your fingertips.

Wrap the dough in greaseproof paper and refrigerate until firm or you are ready to make the biscuits. Roll the dough out on a lightly floured surface to about 3mm thick, cut out circles using a 7cm cookie cutter and place them 2cm apart on baking trays lined with greaseproof paper. Press any trimmings together and reroll to make more biscuits.

Prick all over with a fork, then put the trays in the fridge for 30 minutes. Preheat the oven to 180°C/160°C fan/gas 4 and bake for 15–20 minutes until the biscuits are dry, firm and golden. The longer you cook them for, the crisper they will be (but be careful not to burn them). Transfer to wire racks to cool; when the biscuits first come out of the oven they may be a little fragile, but they will set as they cool. Store in an airtight container.

BAG-FREE, HARM-FREE
ROSEMARY AND SEA SALT POPCORN

In the winter, those long dark Saturday evenings are movie time in our house. It is my favourite night of the week. In times gone by we used to go to the cinema, but it got expensive as our family grew, and anyway, we now think that lighting the fire, curling up on the sofa and having our own choice of film with popcorn we've made ourselves is much more fun. We all snuggle up, and I turn a blind eye to any kernels that get spilled.

Natural, air-popped corn is actually a pretty good snack food, low in fat and sugar- and salt-free, with fibre and antioxidants in the hulls. The problem with the ready-to-eat sort is that the first thing the manufacturers do is douse it in fat, sugar, salt and chemicals. One American report some years back found that a medium-sized serving of movie theatre popcorn had more fat than a breakfast of bacon and eggs, a burger and fries, and a steak dinner....all put together. National Health Service guidelines tell us that the average woman should limit her total fat intake to no more than 70g per day; a medium bag of sweet popcorn from one of the UK's biggest cinema chains has 34.4g of fat: almost half the daily total from one little snack. And if you needed any more persuading: microwave popcorn used to contain an artificial 'butter flavouring' called diacetyl, which is implicated in causing a non-reversible obstructive lung disease illness called 'popcorn lung' (*bronchiolitis obliterans*).

I do understand why my children got so excited when they spotted microwave-in-the-bag popcorn in the supermarket recently. It was in small, neat, brightly coloured packs, covered with fun pictures, promising 'only 80 calories' and instant, no-mess deliciousness. Reading the label, the use of both palm oil and artificial sweeteners concerned me. But what I've also found out is that the packaging becomes a bigger issue, because the popcorn is cooked in it. There are reports that the bag lining is usually coated with perfluorochemicals (PFCs), to stop the popcorn sticking and to help keep the bag dry. Reports suggest that PFCs can stay in the body for long periods of time and are potentially carcinogenic. Since the bag is classed as packaging and not an ingredient, there's no need to declare the PFCs on the label. But I know I wouldn't want my family to eat it.

So I tell my children that together we'll make great popcorn. I tackle the stove bit, they get the bowls ready and the excitement starts as they hear the popping begin.

SERVES » 4

3 small sprigs of fresh rosemary

3 tablespoons olive or rapeseed oil

110g popping corn

60g unsalted butter, melted

½ teaspoon salt

Pull the leaves off the rosemary, chop them finely and discard the stems. Pour the oil into a large, heavy-based saucepan and add the corn. Cover the pot with a lid left very slightly ajar and turn the heat to medium. Shake the pan as the corn pops… this will start in less than a minute. When the popping slows almost to a stop, remove from the heat.

Tip the popcorn into a large serving bowl and drizzle with the melted butter and rosemary, sprinkle with the sea salt and combine well. That's it. It's that simple.

NO CHILD SLAVERY FLOURLESS CHOCOLATE AND ORANGE BROWNIES

Children really love chocolate brownies. Actually, the truth is that everyone loves a good chocolate brownie. Fudgy and warm, baked so that it is crumbly around the outside and still a little gooey in the middle. There is a moment of sheer delight if you can serve them almost direct from the oven, with a scoop of vanilla ice cream on top, so the warmth of the brownie makes the ice cream melt and trickle down. It's just so good, what could possibly spoil such enjoyment?

Well, a closer look at the extent of child labour, even slavery, in cocoa production might do that: children who never have any kind of education or healthcare, because they work 12 or more hours a day and their families are still too poor to send them to school or provide them with even basic medical care. Children exposed to pesticides, with no protective clothing or instruction on how to use chemicals more safely. Children scarred by machete injuries, as they harvest the pods from the trees and get hernias from carrying heavy loads over long distances. All to give us the beans from which cocoa powder and chocolate are made.

Children are being trafficked, beaten, humiliated and abused, and yet this is massively under-reported. Two-thirds of the world's cocoa supply comes from the Côte d'Ivoire and elsewhere in West Africa, where some reports suggest up to 200,000 children are working in conditions that resemble, or in some cases are indeed, slavery. So how do we actively fight against child slavery in the cocoa trade? The single most powerful way is to vote with your wallet. Buying chocolate with traceable origins supports businesses and cooperatives that treat their workers with dignity and respect, and directly supports organisations investing in a fairer future for cacao farmers.

SERVES »12

- 250g dark chocolate (approx. 70 per cent cocoa solids), broken into chunks
- 250g unsalted butter
- 3 medium eggs
- 250g golden caster sugar
- 1 tablespoon orange extract or the zest of 2 oranges
- 300g ground almonds
- pinch of fine sea salt
- 100g white chocolate, broken into chunks

Preheat the oven to 170°C/150°C fan/gas 3, and line a 23cm square baking tin with non-stick baking parchment.

Set a heatproof bowl over a pan of simmering water, making sure the base of the bowl doesn't touch the water and add the dark chocolate and butter. Leave to melt, stirring occasionally, then remove from the heat.

Meanwhile, beat the eggs and sugar together in a mixing bowl. Add the orange extract, mix well, then gradually stir in the melted chocolate. Fold in the ground almonds and salt, followed by the white chocolate chunks. Spoon the mixture into the tin and bake for 25 minutes. Turn off the oven and leave for a further 5 minutes. When you test it with a skewer it should come out sticky but not coated with the raw mixture. If not yet cooked, put the tin back into the oven, turn the heat back on for another few minutes, then test again.

As soon as the brownies are ready, remove from the oven and either leave them to rest briefly if you want to serve them warm, or leave to cool and then put them into the coldest part of the fridge for 1 hour before cutting into squares. Store in an airtight container and if you can resist eating them, they are even nicer the following day.

HELP YOUR LOCAL DAIRY FARMER RICE PUDDING

As the nights draw in, I instinctively start to think about making rice pudding. Sweet, warm and welcoming, the fragrance of slightly burnt milk and spices promises an evening of warmth and love, snuggled up under blankets in front of the fire. It's comfort food.

The price of supermarket milk however, is not giving comfort to farmers. Quite the opposite: these are desperate times. In October 2012, *Farmers Weekly* magazine reported that suicides in the farming industry were running at three times the national average. A series of factors have created this crisis, including long exhausting hours, social isolation, and the sometimes baffling paperwork and bureaucracy of modern farming. But at its heart is an income crisis: in real terms, the price of milk has headed downwards for years and farmers are quite simply not being paid a fair price for what they produce. At times, they are paid less than the cost of production, and it is driving many of them, at the very least, to bankruptcy. When we demand cheaper food, the supermarkets respond by using milk as a loss leader, and the small dairy farmer loses out; and if this war on milk prices continues, then we can expect to see the continued demise of the majority of small family-run farms, and industrialised super-dairies will take over.

There is hope, however. Some family farms are surviving by selling their dairy products under their 'own label' through farm shops and their local markets. If you can buy milk, cream, butter, yogurt or cheese directly, then do, so it supports and protects the farmer, the cows, the countryside and the local community. In this recipe I use milk, cream and butter, so there's a chance for everyone to help their local dairy farmer.

SERVES » 6

1 litre whole milk
100ml double cream
1 teaspoon vanilla powder or 1 vanilla
   pod split lengthways
50g light muscovado sugar
1 bay leaf
½ teaspoon grated nutmeg
pinch of sea salt
60g unsalted butter, cut into small cubes
140g pudding or Arborio rice

Allow about 3 hours' cooking time from start to finish; you can always reheat the pudding if it's ready before dinner, or if you make it in the morning as I sometimes do at the weekend.

Preheat the oven to 180°C/160°C fan/gas 4. Place all the ingredients into a 1.5-litre ovenproof dish, stir well and put it in the oven, then reduce the temperature to 150°C/130°C fan/gas 2. After 30 minutes, open the oven door and stir well, then leave it to cook gently for about a further 1 hour 30 minutes. After 2 hours in total, the pudding may not be set as firmly as you would expect, but remove it from the oven and leave it to stand for 1 hour and it will thicken as the rice continues to absorb the liquid.

Excellent served with plum jam.

100 PER CENT FAIR TRADE CHOCOLATE HONEY TRUFFLES

For the past seven years I've been making truffles with fair trade chocolate for my children, using my friend, Rococo Chocolate founder, Chantal Coady's recipe. They may at first seem like a grown-up and decadent treat for young children, but it helps teach them that you don't have to buy everything that's special: you can make truffles at home. There are no additives, artificial flavourings or preservatives in these truffles and what's more, if you use fair trade ingredients then the farmers and growers should be paid a fair price.

Sadly the same can't be said for all chocolate. The production of cocoa beans for the big name brands still causes deforestation, and even with recent EU legislation that attempts to fight the use of child labour in cocoa farming, the problem is still with us. Furthermore, the labelling of a chocolate bar as 'fair trade' may not guarantee you anything. The largest confectionery companies use a scheme called 'mass balancing'. To put it simply, this means that if 20 per cent of the beans they buy are fair trade, they can label any 20 per cent of their products as such. So you have no idea if the chocolate bar you just bought actually had any fair trade cocoa beans in it, and the scheme is open to manipulation to create an impression that they are doing the right thing, for example by always having the fair trade label on the 20 per cent of their products being most aggressively advertised. So look for organic fair trade chocolate from smaller producers, which will have traceability or a guarantee that all their products are made with fair trade cocoa beans.

MAKES » 50

210g chocolate (ideally 70 per cent
    cocoa solids)
200ml whipping cream
50g runny honey
50g unsalted butter, diced first then
    softened
For coating the truffles
500g good-quality dark or milk
    chocolate
cocoa powder, to finish

Break the chocolate up into pieces and then melt it in a heatproof bowl sitting over a pan of gently simmering water, making sure that the base of the bowl does not touch the water, then set aside. Place the cream and honey in a small heavy-based saucepan. Gently heat until almost boiling, then remove from the heat and leave for a couple of minutes to cool slightly. Spoon about one third of the hot cream into the melted chocolate and stir (a silicone spatula is best for this). Add another third and keep stirring gently as the mixture starts to thicken. As you add the final third you will have a smooth and beautifully glossy emulsion. Next, beat the butter in gently until it is fully incorporated. You can use a stick blender, but be careful not to add any air in.

Pour the chocolate mixture into a shallow ceramic or glass container, spread it evenly with a spatula and place a sheet of clingfilm over the surface. Leave it at room temperature for 1 hour to firm up. Spoon the mixture into a piping bag and pipe truffle-shaped balls onto a baking tray lined with greaseproof paper. You can secure the corners of the paper with a little bit of the chocolate mixture so it doesn't move. Put the truffles into the fridge for 1 hour to firm up.

Melt the coating chocolate as before, then remove the bowl from the pan of water and leave to cool until barely warm but still liquid. Dip the chilled truffles into the chocolate one by one, using a dipping fork. Make sure each one is evenly coated, then roll in cocoa powder. Return to the lined baking tray and leave to set.

These truffles will keep in an airtight container for up to ten days. If you want to give them as presents, place them in cellophane bags to make beautiful gifts.

PUDDINGS AND SWEETS

LOW CO$_2$ SEASONAL BERRY TARTS

These French-style tarts are a showstopper, but there is a condition attached to this recipe: I'd ask you only to make these tarts with fruit that is in season. Out-of-season berries are bland, frozen berries are mushy, and dull raspberries, watery strawberries and flavourless blackberries do not belong on these tarts. But in season, they are the finest fruit; local strawberries are fragrant, blackberries are sweet and raspberries, picked in the summer sun, are so delicious that they make me want to burst into song.

Planting a few fruit bushes and strawberry plants possibly gets you the most delicious fruit. A single mature blackberry bush can produce 4.5–9kg fruit in one season, while strawberries can be grown in borders, containers or even hanging baskets, and can fruit as little as 60 days after planting. But what also matters is that airfreighted fruit means CO$_2$ emissions, which contributes to climate change, and I do not want my tarts to help heat up the planet. Using local fruit in season avoids airfreight, which emits more greenhouse gases per food mile than any other mode of transport.

MAKES ∞ 18 small tarts /cm
(or 2 large tarts 11.5cm)

For the pastry
200g plain flour, plus extra for dusting
140g unsalted butter, diced, plus extra
    for greasing
large pinch of salt
150g ground almonds
50g caster sugar
1 medium egg yolk
For the crème pâtissière filling
6 medium egg yolks
75g caster sugar
20g cornflour
25g plain flour
400ml whole milk
100ml double cream
1 teaspoon vanilla powder or the seeds
    of 2 vanilla pods
For the jam filling
200g raspberries (or berries of
    your choice)
200g granulated sugar
400g seasonal berries, such as
    raspberries, blackberries, blueberries,
    loganberries, blackcurrants,
    redcurrants or strawberries (500g for
    2 large tarts)

To make the pastry, put the flour, butter and salt in a large bowl and mix with your fingertips until it resembles fine breadcrumbs. Stir in the almonds and sugar then mix in the egg yolk until the flour starts to clump together. Tip the mixture onto the worktop and bring together with your hands until it forms a ball. Knead very gently on a lightly floured surface until smooth, then shape into a flat disc. Wrap in clingfilm and chill for 30 minutes or up to four days.

Meanwhile, make the crème pâtissière. In a mixing bowl, whisk together the egg yolks and sugar until pale, then whisk in both the cornflour and flour. Put the milk, cream and vanilla in a large, heavy-based pan and gradually bring to the boil. Remove from the heat, wait for a minute, then pour the milk directly onto the egg mixture, whisking continuously. Return everything to the pan, and bring back to the boil, continuously whisking very gently over a medium heat for no more than 1 minute. Tip back into the mixing bowl, cover the surface of the custard with clingfilm to stop a skin forming and leave to cool. Transfer to the fridge to chill until required.

For the jam filling, put the raspberries and sugar in a heavy-based pan and warm gently until they have liquefied, then boil rapidly for about 3 minutes. Check to see if the jam has set by putting a small blob onto a very cold saucer. Leave for 1 minute, then push your finger through the jam. If it wrinkles but holds its shape, then it is ready; if not, bring it back to the boil for a further 1–2 minutes and test again. It is important not to over-boil the jam as it will lose flavour. Set aside to cool.

Preheat the oven to 200°C/180°C fan/gas 6. Grease the baking tins with a little butter and dust with flour. Roll out the pastry to 3mm thick and cut circles large enough to cover the base and sides of each tin, pushing it firmly into place. Prick the pastry all over with a fork, line with baking parchment and fill with baking beans. Bake for 12 minutes for the smaller tarts and 20–25 minutes for the larger tarts. Remove the baking beans and paper, and bake for a further 2 minutes, then cool the pastry cases in their tins, on a wire rack. Wrap in clingfilm once cold, until you are ready to assemble the tarts.

When you are ready to serve, spread the jam evenly over the base of the pastry, top with the crème pâtissière and scatter liberally with berries. Serve within the hour.

FAIR TRADE VANILLA MADELEINES with baked peaches

Delightful as it is to eat delicate madeleines served with ripe, cooked peaches and whipped cream, there is something equally wonderful in the aroma of the fruit, rum and vanilla cooking; because sometimes the making of a pudding is as delicious as the experience of eating it.

The complex floral aroma reminds me of the Mubuku Moringa Vanilla Farmers' Association in western Uganda. We followed red earth roads through lush green rainforest, just a short distance from the border with the Democratic Republic of Congo. There are children everywhere, and I watch as fresh, just-picked vanilla arrives in sacks and is dropped onto a tarpaulin to be weighed. Everyone is smiling. The farmers chat, laugh and swap gossip, but I soon find out that it wasn't always this way. Until the fair trade cooperative was formed, the vanilla was not good quality, said a farmer standing in front of me. His eyes widened as he explained why: how gangs of men would come over the border to steal the vanilla. They carried sharp, heavy machetes and they meant business; often they would come at night. For those farmers who did try to stand up to the thieves, the consequences were violent. But this was the farmers' cash crop: the money that paid for sending their children to school, buying clothes and meeting medical bills. Losing his vanilla crop would leave a farmer desperate, and his neighbours would become frightened. They would harvest their vanilla as quickly as they could, regardless of whether it was ripe, because some money, even if it was below the cost of production for poorer grades of vanilla, was better than no money at all. Their fear was compounded because the thieves would also attack the vanilla vines, ruining not just one but two seasons' harvest.

But now, the raids have almost stopped because the farmers' cooperative handles the sale of vanilla and the thieves have nowhere to go. So the farmers now have the confidence to leave the vanilla on the vines to ripen; they can earn more for their families from the higher-quality vanilla and they no longer face a constant threat from violent gangs of thieves.

The secret to making perfect madeleines is not to use eggs from the fridge. By using warmer eggs, the whites and yolks combine more easily when you whisk them.

SERVES »4–6

For the madeleines
2 medium eggs, at room temperature
100g caster sugar
1 tablespoon Ndali vanilla extract
juice and zest of 1 lemon
¾ teaspoon baking powder
100g unsalted butter, plus 1 tablespoon melted and cooled slightly
100g '00' flour, plus extra for dusting

For the peaches
4 ripe peaches
2 tablespoons unsalted butter
25g sugar
6–8 tablespoons rum (optional)
whipped or clotted cream, to serve

Warm a mixing bowl with hot water and dry it thoroughly. Whisk the eggs, sugar and vanilla in the bowl until the mixture is fluffy. Lightly whisk in the lemon juice and zest, baking powder, 100g of the butter and the '00' flour. Leave to stand for 20 minutes.

Preheat the oven to 180°C/160°C fan/gas 4, and brush the madeleine tray with the remaining melted butter, then dust with the flour, tapping out any excess. Spoon the mixture gently into the prepared madeleine tray and bake for 8–10 minutes or until the mixture has risen a little in the middle and is fully cooked through. Transfer the madeleines to a wire rack and leave to cool.

Cut the peaches into quarters and remove the stones (peaches have a natural shape which makes them easier to split).

Put the butter, sugar and peach quarters in a saucepan over a low heat and stew, stirring occasionally, for 12–15 minutes. If the peaches are soft, check them after 10 minutes. If they are firm, overcooking them will dry them out, so add a few tablespoons of rum, if necessary. Set aside (the peaches carry on softening). Serve the peaches with the madeleines and whipped cream.

RECLAIM CONTROL CARROT CAKE

I almost bought a carrot cake in my local supermarket last week. It was in a pretty box, and it looked very tempting. I wondered though, what went on behind the carefully designed packaging and the wording meant to convince me to buy it.

I'll be honest: for a product that said it was 'made with the finest organic ingredients', I was surprised to see that it included margarine, coconut, palm oil, palm stearin and palm kernel oil. I have a bee in my bonnet about coconut being used as a cheap 'filler' in many supermarket cakes and desserts. I've even found it in a tiramisu, ruining the flavour. For me, it's just wrong, there or in a carrot cake. And I remembered two reasons why I try not to buy mass-produced cakes.

The first is that, while they have a 'best before' or 'sell by' date, they never show the date they were made. All too often, supermarket cakes are what I call 'soft but stale': not fresh, in fact days or possibly weeks old, but made with emulsifiers, humectants and 'modified' ingredients, included to give that long-lasting softness. And secondly: if there was ever a time in my life when I didn't care about what was in the food I ate, I'm over it now. I want to know what I'm eating, and when it comes to cakes, the best way is to make it myself. That also means I'm not sending unrecyclable packaging to landfill, or spending my money on something that leaves me disappointed. Most of all, choosing the ingredients means I can take another step towards supporting sustainable farming and fair trade products. There are hidden costs in so much 'cheap' food, and the only way to avoid this trap is to look beyond the marketing and hype, and reclaim power over what you eat.

SERVES » 8

100g unrefreshed 1-week-old
    sourdough starter (see page 41
    and page 192)
145ml sunflower oil
4 tablespoons golden syrup
    finely grated zest of 3 oranges,
    plus 100ml juice
225g light soft brown sugar
3 medium eggs
200g carrots, grated
100g pistachios, finely chopped
225g plain flour
3 teaspoons baking powder
2 teaspoons Ndali vanilla powder
1 teaspoon freshly grated nutmeg
For the cream cheese frosting
75g unsalted butter, at room
    temperature
150g icing sugar
525g full-fat cream cheese, at room
    temperature
1½ teaspoons Ndali vanilla extract
zest of 2 oranges
To decorate
50g pistachios, chopped
1½ teaspoons pink peppercorns, crushed

Line the bases of three 20cm round cake tins with non-stick baking paper. Preheat the oven to 180°C/160°C fan/gas 4.

In a large mixing bowl, beat the sourdough starter, oil, golden syrup, orange zest and sugar together until smooth.

In a separate bowl, beat the eggs until pale and frothy, and fold them into the oil and sugar mixture, then stir in the orange juice, carrots and pistachios.

Sift the flour, baking powder, vanilla powder and nutmeg together. Fold the dry mixture into the wet mixture, ensuring it is fully incorporated. Divide the mixture evenly between the tins and bake for 18–25 minutes or until a light golden colour and a skewer inserted into each cake comes out clean. Remove from the oven and leave to cool in the tins.

While the cakes are cooling, make the frosting. Put the butter, icing sugar, cream cheese, vanilla and orange zest into a bowl and stir with a wooden spoon until the mixture becomes a paste. Then whisk using a hand-held or electric whisk until smooth and thoroughly blended.

When the cakes are completely cool, place one layer on a serving plate and spread with one-third of the icing. Then place the second layer of sponge on this, and spread with another third of the frosting. Finally, put the final layer in place, and spread the remaining frosting over the top. Decorate the cake with a scattering of pistachios and pink peppercorns.

DON'T THROW OLD BANANAS AWAY CARAMEL BANANA LOAF

I am a huge fan of bananas, but modern farming practices leave me uneasy. Often their cultivation involves deforestation, the heavy use of toxic pesticides and very poor wages and conditions for estate workers, but increasingly, we are now able to buy 'sustainable' bananas that meet social, economic and environmental standards. Luckily they keep well and travel by boat, and they don't need any plastic packaging: it makes me mad to see them wrapped in plastic bags in the supermarket.

Bananas are one of the most successful fair trade products, on our shelves for over 20 years now and widely available. In his book *How Bad Are Bananas?*, Mike Berners-Lee points out that compared to its carbon footprint, you get a whole lot of nutritional value from a product that is grown in sunshine and not a greenhouse. That is, as long as you actually eat them. An estimated three out of ten bananas are thrown away. Let's see now: we pick the fruit, transport it to a warehouse, then take it 5,000 miles across the sea to another warehouse, before it goes to the supermarket, into your trolley, home in your car, and finally into your fruit bowl. Where a few days later it turns a bit brown so you chuck it in the bin? You can't honestly read that without realising that this is something you need to change.

You can use overripe bananas in smoothies and ice creams, but my favourite way to use them is in this banana loaf. I've slightly tweaked the spices and added caramel sauce, but the original recipe is from Stones Bakery in Falmouth, Cornwall. It is dark, sweet, moist and very banana-ry indeed.

MAKES » 900g LOAF

200g unsalted butter

300g brown sugar

1 tablespoon Ndali vanilla powder

1 teaspoon freshly grated nutmeg

3 eggs

300g plain flour

3 teaspoons bicarbonate of soda

60g buttermilk

6 bananas

125g pecans or walnuts

For the caramel sauce

50ml water

150g granulated sugar

30ml golden syrup

100ml double cream

40g unsalted butter

Line the base and sides of a 900g loaf tin with non-stick baking paper, to stand about 3cm above the rim of the tin, then preheat the oven to 160°C/140°C fan/gas 2½.

Put the butter, sugar, vanilla powder and nutmeg in a bowl, and using an electric mixer, whisk on high until pale and creamy. Add the eggs one at a time, then the flour and bicarbonate of soda, mixing them in well. Then add the buttermilk and mix again. Lightly mash the bananas and chop the pecans, then fold them through the cake mixture to combine. Pour into the prepared tin, then cover the top of the cake with foil to protect it from catching and burning. Bake for 1 hour 15 minutes–1 hour 25 minutes (depending on how large and ripe your bananas are, which will change the baking time). Use a skewer to test – it should come out with barely a crumb attached when inserted into the middle of the loaf. Leave to cool in the tin.

Next, make the caramel sauce. Put the water, sugar and golden syrup into a deep, heavy-based saucepan, stir just until the sugar has dissolved, then bring to the boil over a high heat without stirring, cooking until the mixture is a caramel colour – about 7–10 minutes. Meanwhile, in a separate pan, bring the cream almost to the boil. Remove the caramel syrup from the heat and pour the cream into the pan. It will be very hot and bubble ferociously, so please be careful. Whisk until smooth then stir in the butter.

Remove the cake from the tin and poke about 40 holes into the top using the skewer. Pour the warm caramel sauce over the top of the cake and leave to cool before serving.

SOUR MILK SCONES

Milk is cheap. It is so cheap these days that people don't give a thought to pouring milk down the drain when it starts to 'turn', which is a shame on so many levels. Sour milk makes excellent scones. The acidity reacts with the raising agent in the flour to give a better rise and lighter scone, but the true cost of cheap milk actually leaves a very sour taste.

I cannot imagine that anyone went into their local supermarket and demanded cheap milk. Who would stand at customer services saying that they don't care about cows or their welfare, and that they really don't give a toss about what is in the milk as long as it's cheap? Was it you? Because it certainly wasn't me.

It's time we faced the reality that there is no such thing as cheap milk, as the price we make others pay is an altogether heavier one. The persistent low market price for milk is leading to large farming companies looking for the lowest possible cost of production, by proposing and building mega dairies, where thousands of cows are housed in enormous sheds, never going outside.

Mega-dairies are a tragedy in the making. In the USA, they have been implicated in the routine use of antibiotics on a massive scale, encouraging the development of drug-resistant bacteria which can spread from animals to humans. To grow the enriched diet these indoor cattle need, more land and more water is used, and that land is sprayed with chemical fertilisers, herbicides, pesticides and fungicides, before being given one last blast of glyphosate before the feed is harvested. The true cost of cheap milk is a system which profits the global petrochemical, chemical and pharmaceutical industries, that pollutes the earth and contributes further to global warming.

By comparison, the average British dairy herd had just 75 cows in 2000 (and is about 115 now), with access to seasonal pasture and fresh air, and the ability to move and exercise. And if you ever saw cows arrive in a field full of fresh spring grass, you'd see their reaction. They leap about like crazy, happy things, bucking and bellowing with joy. Not so the animals that are kept indoors for all of their lives without seeing daylight.

To quote Compassion in World Farming, cows belong in fields, not confined in gigantic sheds. As we move away from the bad times of battery hens, let's not instead be faced with battery cows. When you buy milk, think about what you are putting in your basket; and be prepared to use it, not pour it away.

MAKES » 8

225g self-raising flour, plus extra
    for dusting
75g unsalted butter, chilled and diced
¼ teaspoon sea salt
50g caster sugar
100g unrefreshed 1-week-old
    sourdough starter (optional –
    see page 41 and page 192)
125ml grass-fed sour whole milk,
    possibly a drop more
1 tablespoon fresh lemon juice
1 egg, beaten with 1 tablespoon milk,
    for the glaze
fresh cream and raspberry jam, to serve

Preheat the oven to 200°C/180°C fan/gas 6. Put the flour, butter, salt and sugar into a bowl and mix together thoroughly. Make a well in the centre. In a large jug, whisk the sourdough starter (if using), sour milk and lemon juice together then pour this into the centre of the dry mixture. Lightly knead the mixture together to form a dough. If it seems a bit dry, add a little more milk, a few drops at a time; if it is too sticky, then add a dusting of flour so you can handle it more easily.

Turn out onto a floured work surface and pat the dough out with your hands to 2.5cm thick. Cut into rounds or squares (or even triangles), depending on your preference, and put them on a baking tray. Remember that the trick to really lovely scones is to handle the dough as little and as lightly as possible. Glaze the scones with the beaten egg and bake for 18–20 minutes until golden on top and risen.

Leave to cool on a wire rack, then wrap in a linen cloth. If you want to freeze these scones, do so as soon as they are cool. Scones are normally best enjoyed the same day, but if you use the sourdough starter in these, then the lactic acid helps preserve them and they are just as lovely the next day.

A VERY ETHICAL AND EXTREMELY DELICIOUS CHOCOLATE CAKE

This chocolate cake is not just easy to make: it's also delectable, and 'just'. This cake is where all my principles meet. It is a slice of pure chocolatey fairness, and the result is magic.

As I stir Mott Green's melted zero-carbon Grenada chocolate and it meets Ndali's intense organic fair trade vanilla powder there are bursts of deliciousness and, for me, emotion. There is an intense feeling of connection to the farmers who grow the vanilla and the Ugandan workers who laugh and sing and chat while they process it. At the same time I can almost hear Mott's New York accent describing how each stage of the chocolate-making process is integral to the end result and I recall the aroma of the chocolate factory. I remember the flames, roaring across the cocoa bean roaster, and the relaxed pride and smiles of the Grenadian cocoa farmers that I met.

Every ingredient in this cake is fair in its own right: a tribute to the farmers that produced all the ingredients. Not just the growers in Uganda and Grenada or the small farmers producing fair trade sugar, but my local farmers too. The heritage flour I use is grown in the next county to me, without pesticides or chemical fertilisers, and it is milled on the farm; the eggs were collected warm this morning from my own chickens: the nutmeg that I grate was bought directly from the cooperative farmers I met on the Spice Islands. Even the baking powder I use is organic, with organic butter from St Helens farm in York, and pure sea salt from Halen Môn.

It may be that your version of this cake will be different to mine. It might even be that you can use just one ingredient that states its fairness, but whether you are a farmer or a baker, there is joy and pride in producing something yourself.

SERVES » 10-12

100g dark chocolate (approx. 85 per cent cocoa solids)

250g unsalted butter, plus extra for greasing

125 caster sugar

125g dark muscovado sugar

4 large eggs

1 teaspoon baking powder

60g cocoa powder

175g plain flour (I like to use a heritage grain such as Rivet, Einkorn or Emmer), plus extra for dusting

pinch of sea salt

1 teaspoon grated nutmeg

1 teaspoon vanilla powder

3 tablespoons unrefreshed 1-week-old sourdough starter (see page 41 and page 192) or rapeseed oil

50g white chocolate

50g dark chocolate (approx. 70 per cent cocoa solids)

Preheat the oven to 150°C/130°C fan/gas 2. Grease and flour a 23cm round cake tin. Break the dark chocolate into pieces and melt it gently in a heatproof bowl over a pan of simmering water, making sure the base of the bowl does not touch the water, then leave to cool slightly.

In a large bowl, cream the butter, caster and muscovado sugars together. Stir in the melted chocolate, making sure it's not too hot or it will melt the butter. Add the eggs and mix well. Sift the remaining dry ingredients together and add them to the mixture.

Beat with an electric hand-held mixer on full power for about 5 minutes, mixing the sourdough starter or oil in completely just before you finish, and transfer to the prepared baking tin. Cover with tin foil and bake for 25 minutes, then remove the foil and bake for a further 25–30 minutes. This long, slow, gentle bake ensures that the cake does not burn and almost 'sets'. Please don't overbake it.

Leave the cake to cool in the tin. To serve, melt the white chocolate and dark chocolate separately, in heatproof bowls over a pan of simmering water. Do not allow the water to touch the base of the bowl, but let the steam warm the base and stir gently until the chocolate is melted. Drizzle the melted chocolate in a zigzag pattern over the cake and serve.

LOVE THE MIDGES CHOCOLATE AND BANANA MUFFINS

Fair trade chocolate and banana make an excellent combination, and this is another great way to use up your leftover ripe fruit. These sweet, American-style, crumble-topped muffins are easy and quick to make, and with very little effort, give you a way to support the environment and ultimately the lungs of the planet.

Standing in a plantation with banana plants stretching up above the cocoa trees, Mott Green, of the Grenada Chocolate Company, explained to me that these two species, from different continents, do make amazing partners. The banana trees provide the ideal home for beneficial insects, and the cocoa husks add nutrients and bulk to the forest floor that help sustain the young banana trees.

But what does this have to do with you and these delicious muffins? Well, everything, according to Mott. What we decide to buy affects demand. So many of the farmers who produce our bananas and cocoa beans are under financial pressure to grow more for less money, he tells me. 'A farm I once visited stripped the forest floor, planted nothing but cocoa trees and fed them a noxious cocktail of chemically-produced fertilisers. It was an ecological disaster. A monoculture, and the farmers sat back and waited for their bumper crop. It never came. Not one cocoa pod; because they had stripped away the habitat of the midges that pollinate the cocoa flowers.' So you see, when you buy ethically produced chocolate you can support individual farmers, who tend their crops in ways that support the natural fertility of the plants. It is through small communities, cooperatives and fair trading practices that farmers get a decent price for their cocoa. Take away that fair price, and the farmers either turn to other crops to feed their families or are driven towards chemical fertilisers, monoculture and the less fertile methods of the large-scale cocoa plantation. Ultimately, that will drive up the cost of cocoa, but at what cost to the environment?

MAKES »12 MUFFINS

For the crumble topping
2 tablespoons golden granulated sugar
2 heaped tablespoons plain flour
2 tablespoons cocoa powder
50g unsalted butter, diced
For the muffins
275g self-raising flour
140g light brown sugar
½ teaspoon salt
1 teaspoon Ndali vanilla powder
1 teaspoon baking powder
75g milk chocolate buttons
60g cocoa powder
100g unrefreshed 1-week-old
    sourdough starter (optional –
    see page 41 and page 192)
2 bananas, sliced
120ml rapeseed oil
260ml whole milk
2 medium eggs

To make the crumble topping, sift the dry ingredients together in a bowl, then rub in the butter, until the mixture resembles breadcrumbs. Keep this ready to sprinkle over the muffins just before they go into the oven.

Preheat the oven to 180°C/160°C fan/gas 4.

Stir all the dry ingredients for the muffins together in a mixing bowl. Add the sourdough starter (if using), bananas, oil, milk and eggs, and mix just enough to combine. It is important not to overmix the ingredients as this will result in the gluten being activated and you will get a tough muffin.

Divide the mixture between tulip-shaped muffin cases in a 12-hole muffin tin. Sprinkle evenly with the crumble topping, then bake for 20–25 minutes until firm. Leave to cool on a wire rack.

WINDFALL PEARS WITH PANNA COTTA

One afternoon, my eldest daughter ran into the kitchen, her eyes shining and her blonde hair wild. 'Look!' she called out, tipping a dozen windfall pears out of her school bag onto the kitchen table. 'I found these in the old school orchard.'

As we cut some up to share, I realised I'd never tasted such glorious pears. They were sweeter and firmer than the ones found in the supermarket. I wondered what variety they were and how many pears one tree could produce. Days later, I talked to David Morris, the head gardener of the National Fruit Collection at Brogdale in Kent, and he explained that fruit trees are grafted onto different root stocks. After seven years, a tree grafted onto a dwarf rootstock will produce up to 30kg of fruit; on a quince rootstock, 50kg; and on a *Pyrus Communis* rootstock, up to 120kg. The horticultural curator of the Brogdale Collections, Lorinda Jewsbury, told me that 'Although we have over 3,000 varieties of fruit trees here, we keep just two of each. Trees are alive and you never want to think about losing any, so we encourage the public to grow heritage varieties in their gardens, because you never know if we might lose a tree here and we don't want that genetic material to be lost'.

The Brogdale Collections is an essential resource. As climate change affects the natural conditions that commercial fruit trees are used to, new pests and diseases appear. The National Fruit Collection provides a reference for varieties that might be more robust and better at fighting these new diseases and pests.

Trees provide a wonderful resource for wildlife; they convert the CO_2 we produce into the oxygen we breath and they provide us with fabulous fruit from our gardens. If you have even a small amount of space, invest in the future. Plant a tree.

SERVES » 6

6 small sheets of leaf gelatine
500ml double cream
500ml buttermilk
1 big Ndali vanilla pod, split lengthways,
    or 1 teaspoon vanilla extract
100g golden caster sugar
100ml Irish whiskey
For the toffee pears
3 large firm pears
30g unsalted butter
100g caster sugar
100g soft brown sugar

For the panna cotta, soak the gelatine in room-temperature water for 5 minutes until soft.

Meanwhile, pour the cream and buttermilk into a heavy-based pan, add the vanilla, golden caster sugar and whiskey and stir over a moderate heat until the sugar has dissolved. Remove from the heat and leave to stand for 2 minutes.

Give the gelatine leaves a good squeeze and shake off any excess water, then drop them into the hot cream and sugar. Leave them for a few seconds, then whisk until the gelatine dissolves. Leave the mixture to stand for 45 minutes at room temperature, stirring occasionally, then remove the vanilla pod (if using).

As the liquid thickens, strain it through a fine sieve into a jug, to remove any lumps then pour into six 125ml dariole moulds or small teacups. Chill overnight or until thoroughly set.

About 25–30 minutes before you are ready to serve, cook the pears. Preheat the oven to 170°C/150°C fan/gas 3. Slice the pears in half and put them, cut-side down, in a large, heavy-based frying pan with the butter and sugars. (You may have to do this in two batches if your pan is not large enough.) Cook over a high heat for about 5 minutes until the base of each pear is golden brown and the sugar and butter have become a light toffee colour. Transfer the pears and syrup to a lightly buttered ovenproof dish and roast for 8–10 minutes or until tender.

Meanwhile, dip each panna cotta-filled mould into a bowl of hot water for just 10 seconds, then run a sharp knife carefully around the edge and turn out onto a plate, positioning it off-centre (or simply serve in the teacups). Place half a roasted pear next to it, and finish with a drizzle of warmed caramelised juice from the baking dish.

PACKAGING-FREE GOOSEBERRY CRUMBLE

There is a battered enamel tin on my kitchen table. It was my grandmother's and it is full of gooseberries destined for the most comforting and satisfying crumble. They have spilled over and onto the table as though trying to escape their fate; but they will end up in a classic pudding that is a remarkably effective in making use of local, seasonal fruit, avoiding food miles and packaging waste.

My grandmother's generation would make crumbles in tins and dishes like this one, and just like this recipe, they would have a crunchy topping with fruit and sugary juices bubbling through the cracks, served piping hot with a huge jug of sweet vanilla custard. My brother and I would vie for grandma's attention, to be given the most topping.

Less than twenty-five years after she died, it seems almost unbelievable that so many people buy factory-produced crumble. Homemade crumbles are so easy to make, inexpensive and delicious, yet looking at the ready-meal section of my local supermarket, it's obvious that there's enough demand for the commercially produced ones to make them a profitable product. I wonder at what point people gave up on making crumble and surrendered to these mass-produced, shrink-wrapped, plastic-packaged microwavable excuses for a pudding?

This recipe doesn't take much time to make and you can always double the quantities and make two crumbles at the same time, as they freeze brilliantly, keeping for up to three months in the freezer. What's more, I promise that your own homemade crumbles will be so darn good that you will never again buy a commercially produced one.

SERVES » 6

750g gooseberries or Worcester berries, topped and tailed
60g caster sugar
50g locally sourced honey (a dark honey works best if possible)
250g plain flour
75g demerara sugar
25g granulated sugar
pinch of sea salt
100g unsalted butter, diced and chilled, plus extra for greasing
vanilla custard, to serve

Grease a 26 x 20cm tin or heatproof dish with a little butter, spread the gooseberries evenly over the base, scatter with sugar and drizzle with the honey.

Mix the flour, demerara and granulated sugars and salt together, then rub in the butter with your fingers to make a coarse and slightly rough topping. Do not mix with a machine as the result will be too fine. Spread the crumble topping evenly over the fruit, keeping it as light as possible.

When you are ready to bake, preheat the oven to 180°C/160°C fan/gas 4 and bake for 45–50 minutes, until the topping is golden and the gooseberries are bubbling.

Leave the crumble to rest for 10 minutes before serving with lashings of custard.

ORPHANAGE STAR ANISE AND ORANGE BREAD AND BUTTER PUDDING

I can't smell star anise without picturing a ten-year-old boy I sat with at the Blue Dragon orphanage in Hanoi. His father was an alcoholic (homemade stills and alcoholism are quite common in rural Vietnam, and rice is fermented into very strong hooch, a huge social problem in village communities). Somehow this boy had lost the family cow he was in charge of, and in fear of a beating from his father, he ran away and was persuaded to get on a bus by a stranger who promised to help find his home. Four hours later he was, instead, taken to a factory in Hanoi and severely beaten with a bamboo stick as his introduction to life as a child slave labourer. Worse followed and he ran away again. Failing to find food or water, he collapsed and was found by local children with rats running over him, starving and unconscious in a filthy backstreet gutter just a few hundred yards from the orphanage.

I listened while he explained in earnest that he had to get home, as though I, a white-skinned, blue-eyed stranger, might somehow know where he had come from. He explained that it was harvest time and he was needed to help his mother: it was his job to climb the star anise trees to pick the unripe fruit. He was worried about how she would manage without him, but he didn't know the name of his village. It was always simply called 'the village' and no one had ever told him its name. He remembered a sign that pointed towards the village, but he could not decipher it because no one had ever taught him to read.

This recipe uses up leftover bread with butter and marmalade, and sweet star anise from a fair trade producer in northern Vietnam. The cooperative supports an education programme, and in the simplest of terms when you support fair trade you can help provide opportunities for education.

SERVES »10-12

5 star anise
750ml whole milk
600g stale white bread
100g unsalted butter
125g raisins
75g caster sugar
300ml single cream
4 medium eggs
zest of 2 oranges
3–4 tablespoons orange marmalade
300ml double cream, whipped with 1 heaped tablespoon icing sugar, to serve

The night before you want to make the pudding, put the star anise and milk in a small saucepan and heat to just below boiling point. Transfer to a container and leave to cool overnight in the fridge. The following day, strain the milk and reserve the star anise to garnish the pudding.

Preheat the oven to 180°C/160°C fan/gas 4.

Slice the bread into 1.5cm thick slices, butter them and arrange them in a very large, deep dish, scattering the raisins and most of the sugar evenly between each layer (reserve 3–4 tablespoons of sugar to use later). You should get about three layers, depending on the size of your dish. Bear in mind you need to leave a little room at the top, as the pudding will puff up as it cooks.

Put the milk, cream, eggs and half the orange zest in a jug and whisk until evenly combined. Pour this gently over the bread, making sure the liquid is distributed throughout. Set aside for 1 hour to allow the liquid to fully soak into the bread.

Sprinkle the remaining sugar and reserved star anise over the top and pop into the oven. After 1 hour 20 minutes check that the pudding is risen and golden. If it is not golden, cook for a further 10 minutes and check again that it's set in the middle.

Remove from the oven and glaze by gently and evenly spreading the marmalade over the top, while the pudding is still hot. Serve with a dollop of sweetened whipped cream and a scattering of the remaining orange zest.

WINDFALL APPLES__ *The Russet, Crab or Gala red, the Bramley sharp and sweet,* fall almost as if from the sky, landing softly at my feet. *The windfall ones are sweeter than those on the branches high,* and they simply need picking up and turning into pie.

ORGANIC WINDFALL APPLE PIE

I've been picking windfall apples today. They are on an old tree that is perhaps a hundred years old. It is not certified as organic, but I don't think it has ever seen any chemicals. The apples have a natural beauty and make this sweet, wholesome pie, which for all its Englishness could still be taken for an all-American cultural icon. With a golden all-butter pastry and a warm, cinnamon-infused filling, it is good old-fashioned, honest food. Honesty, though, is the last thing that the chemical giants want. For the fourth year in a row, apples topped the USA's 2014 'Dirty Dozen' list, as the most pesticide-contaminated fruit, in the report of the Environmental Working Group, a watchdog organisation in Washington, D.C.

Glyphosate is one of the most widely used herbicides in apple orchards, and one that has been promoted as a safe and environmentally benign product that breaks down in the soil, but recent reports have begun to challenge this assertion. The *Guardian* reported that the World Health Organization's International Agency for Research on Cancer said that glyphosate, the active ingredient in Monsanto's Roundup herbicide, was classified as 'probably carcinogenic to humans'. So I am rephrasing the old adage: 'An apple a day keeps the doctor away: but not if it is covered in herbicide.'

SERVES » 6–8

4 large cooking apples
3 small sweet dessert apples
40g unsalted butter
150g soft brown sugar
1½ teaspoons mixed spice
1 apple, peeled, cored and grated
For the pastry
400g white spelt flour, plus extra
    for dusting
1½ tablespoons baking powder
50g granulated sugar
pinch of sea salt
220g unsalted butter, diced
    and fridge cold
3 egg yolks
To finish
1 egg beaten with 1 tablespoon milk,
    to glaze
To serve
whipped cream or vanilla ice cream

Peel and core the apples. Cut as much flesh as you can from around the core (don't worry if it is in little bits as it will all mix in as it cooks), and dice into bite-sized chunks. Melt the butter and sauté the apple chunks briefly, adding the sugar, mixed spice and grated apple, and cook for 5 minutes more until the grated apple is mushy but the chunks are still not quite cooked. Taste and add more sugar if required. Strain off any excess liquid and set aside.

Preheat the oven to 170°C/150°C fan/gas 3

To make the pastry, put the flour, baking powder, sugar and salt in a mixing bowl, add the butter and rub it in until the mixture resembles breadcrumbs. Stir in the egg yolks and 3 tablespoons of very cold water and mix to a smooth paste. You may need to add another tablespoon or so of water, but only if the dough seems too dry and crumbly: don't make the mixture too wet. Take half the pastry and, handling it lightly, roll it out onto a well-floured surface, into a circle large enough to line the base and sides of a traditional 23cm apple pie tin. Then line the pastry case with non-stick baking paper, fill with baking beans, and blind bake for 12 minutes.

Remove from the oven, carefully remove the paper and baking beans, then spoon in the apples, patting them down to form a flattish, well-packed layer. Roll out the remaining pastry to about 3mm thick on a well-floured surface, then cut it into strips about 1–1.5cm wide and weave these over the top of the apples in a lattice pattern. Brush the strips with eggwash and return the pie to the oven for a further 15–20 minutes. Leave to cool then serve with whipped cream or ice cream.

GROW YOUR OWN FLOWERS__**There has been a revolution in local, seasonal and sustainable food in recent years** and I see absolutely no reason that the same can't be applied to the cut flower industry. But even buying local seasonal flowers has an environmental cost, so for truly ethical flowers plant repeat flowering varieties, such as sweet peas or roses like 'The Generous Gardener'.

SUSTAINABLE STRAWBERRY, VANILLA AND ROSE BUFFALO MILK ICE CREAM

The arrival of strawberries in my garden each year excites me. I have wild alpine strawberries that were, I suspect, brought in by a passing bird decades ago. They grow everywhere, between the lords-and-ladies (wild arum), in the stone walls, under the fruit bushes and along the driveway. They are small, sweet, juicy, highly aromatic and just slightly tart. I can honestly say that I never eat strawberries out of season as they are a disappointment – so I gorge on them when they are around, not least because their perfect state is so fleeting. Not ripe enough, and they are un-perfumed and taste of nothing; and overripe, they simply lose their texture. Strawberries are best served warm from the summer sun – left to ripen on their own, they will develop a deep sweetness and it is at this point you want to capture the moment and devour them. If you have a glut, then seize the opportunity and catch these exquisite berries' most heavenly moment in ice cream, emphasising their sublime charm with rose and vanilla.

This recipe, however is not just about eating strawberries in season, it is also about using buffalo milk, which aside from making really delicious ice cream is also a sustainable product. Although buffalos produce less milk than domestic cows, during the summer months they live happily on much more marginal land, without the need for cereal-based 'concentrate' to supplement their diet, which makes them a much more sustainable choice for pastoral farming on land that is not ideal for domestic cows. Buffalo milk is also higher in fat and in minerals such as calcium, magnesium, potassium and phosphorus but lower in cholesterol than cow's milk, so it's ideal for making the creamiest ice cream, as well as your own yogurt or cottage cheese.

In this recipe, I've recommended using vanilla sugar: caster sugar, stored in a jar with used split vanilla pods, which lend their fragrance to the sugar. Make sure your roses have not been sprayed with pesticides or insecticides.

MAKES »1.2 LITRES
(serves 8)

700ml buffalo milk
5 egg yolks
145g vanilla sugar
4 fresh roses or 3–4 drops of rose extract (attar of roses)
425g fresh strawberries

The day before you want your ice cream, put the buffalo milk, egg yolks and sugar in a heavy-based saucepan and stir over a moderate heat. Keep the liquid moving using a whisk. (If you don't have vanilla sugar, use regular caster sugar with a small vanilla pod split lengthways.)

Keep stirring as the custard thickens. This can take 20–25 minutes, so take your time and don't be tempted to heat it quickly (you'll get scrambled eggs!). The mixture will thicken. When the custard easily coats the back of a spoon, remove it from the heat and scrape it into a clean bowl.

Pluck the rose petals, discarding any that are bruised, and check them for any tiny insects, then stir them into the custard. Leave to cool (I keep my custard in the fridge overnight for the flavour to infuse but if you are in a hurry, use rose extract instead).

Hull the strawberries and blend to a pulp in a food processor. Sieve the custard into the strawberries, discarding the rose petals. Blend the mixture; you can make the ice cream right away, or store the liquid in the fridge in a clean airtight container for up to two days before freezing.

Either follow the manufacturers' instructions if you are using an ice-cream maker, or if you are doing it by hand, pour the mixture into a shallow freezer-proof container and freeze for at least 3 hours, taking it out and whisking it three or four times, at 45-minute intervals to prevent ice crystals forming. Use a timer to remind you, as I often forget to do this!

DRINKS

WHILE THERE'S STILL TIME COFFEE FRAPPÉ

Over the next 50 years, the world coffee crop is going to come under pressure from climate change. It isn't just the direct effect of higher temperatures (above 23°C, the plant's yield and berry quality start to decline) and rainfall patterns being increasingly polarised between long droughts and then intense storms, pests and plant diseases actually benefit from global warming. Insects like the coffee borer beetle are moving into areas that were previously too cool for them and aren't affected by chemical pesticides, while the temperature-sensitive coffee rust fungus has become endemic in places where it was previously unknown.

The other problem for coffee farmers is the lack of genetic diversity in commercial plantings. The coffee we drink comes from two related species, *Coffea arabica* (c.75 per cent of world production) and *Coffea canephora* (or *robusta*: the remaining 25 per cent), and cultivated arabica has a particularly narrow genetic base, which has left it lacking in resistance to pests and diseases. This is largely because the plants in cultivation come from a limited number of ancestors, and have been spread through cuttings and cloning. However, there is some hope. Wild *C. arabica* is native to Ethiopia and parts of Sudan, and was taken from there to Yemen, and in those locations, there is far more genetic diversity, which it may be possible to breed into the commercial plants. But even in its home, climate change, allied to deforestation, poses a significant risk to the coffee crop.

I must admit: I've had more than a moment of selfishly realising that one day I might not get my early-morning brew, but the real problem is what this means for the 25 million rural households across the world who depend on coffee farming for their income. Those farmers are not just statistics, they are people, with real families and hopes and dreams like you and me. So what do we do? I think that in the short term, by supporting fair trade cooperatives of small farmers who cultivate and harvest some of the more unusual strains of arabica coffee, and moving away from the four multinationals that dominate the world coffee trade, there's a chance that we can help to preserve some genetic diversity. In the longer term, we must reinforce our resolve to fight climate change. And when more resistant coffee plants are developed, we must make sure that they are made available to small farmers and don't become the intellectual property of a global agribusiness, or are only made available to vassals of the big coffee companies.

This recipe for a coffee frappé is great if you have an unusual fair trade coffee and want to make the most of its complex flavour. It's also a delicious and easy way to use up any coffee that has gone cold.

SERVES » 4

400ml strong cold coffee
200ml sweetened condensed milk
2 scoops of vanilla ice cream
½ teaspoon vanilla powder or
    2 teaspoons vanilla extract
a small handful of ice cubes, crushed in
    a bag with a rolling pin
To serve
1 tablespoon icing sugar
1 tablespoon cocoa

Put the coffee, condensed milk, ice cream, vanilla and ice cubes in a blender and whizz on full speed for 45 seconds–1 minute. Pour into tall, cold glasses.

Mix the icing sugar and cocoa powder together, and dust this over the surface of each filled glass, using a tea strainer or tiny sieve, as you serve them. If your coffee is not strong enough, or already has milk in it, add 1 teaspoon of instant coffee per person to intensify the flavour before you make the frappé.

GOOD AGRICULTURAL PRACTICE SWEET MANGO AND HONEY LASSI

One of my sweetest memories is sitting on a beach on the island of Ko Phi Phi in Thailand in the evening sun, eating fresh mangoes. They were luscious, fragrant and just the best mangoes I have ever eaten. Rarely in the UK do I ever find one that comes close to that; occasionally, one of the Alphonso variety that we get in late spring might do it. They remind me of golden goose eggs, and I simultaneously feel both delight and a slight guilt from wondering how far it was from being ethically grown. But not buying mangos is also a decision that has an impact, because often they are cultivated by subsistence farmers that sell mangoes as a vital cash crop.

Finding a fresh, ripe fair trade mango is quite a tough job. There are some sources: for example in western India, the Devgad Taluka Mango Growers Co-operative has an extensive programme that supports farmers growing Alphonso mangoes. It's owned by the farmers, with profits distributed to them rather than to company directors or a multinational holding company, according to a study by The George Washington University School of Business. At the other end of the spectrum, organisations like Global G.A.P (Good Agricultural Practice) provide farmers with independent certification that they have met standards for sustainable production, safety and welfare, which can open doors to supplying major retailers in Europe and beyond.

Here in the UK, there's a company called Blue Skies that imports ready-prepared fruit processed in factories close to where it was grown, avoiding chemical agents by using sun-ripened fruit and composting the by-products. Trading with farmers in Ghana since 1998, the company is able, in return, to support development projects, providing schoolrooms and clean water, and helping to secure rural employment in a society that was seeing significant drift to the cities.

A simple and delicious way to use up any leftover ripe or ready-prepared mango is to blend it into a traditional Indian drink called lassi, which I think is perfect with a curry, or just as a smoothie any time of day.

SERVES » 3–4

300g diced mango (about 2–3 peeled
   and de-stoned whole mangoes)
500g homemade yogurt (page 199)
   or plain thick Greek-style yogurt
2–3 tablespoons honey
a good pinch of freshly ground
   cardamom

To make the lassi, simply put all the ingredients in a blender, whizz them together on full, and serve immediately.

ALL NATURAL MILKSHAKES

Suggest making milkshakes to a child and you'll see their happiness. Cold, sweet, frothy and creamy, the only argument in my house would be about the flavour. The most popular choices are either strawberry if it's summer, made with fruit freshly picked from the garden; vanilla at any time of year; or chocolate, with a good dollop of treacly organic barley malt added. I use locally produced milk, fair trade cocoa powder and organic vanilla ice cream, because I want to know what's going into that glass.

It is difficult, though, to resist the pressure to buy them milkshakes sometimes when we're out and about. I won't lie, my children would love to have the ones they've seen advertised, especially if they come from fast-food chains. I can't blame them; after all, millions of pounds are spent on developing flavours designed to appeal to a child's palate, that are then manufactured using chemicals, sugar and cheap corn syrup, and packaged by teams of marketing experts skilled in manipulating a child's desire to guzzle these highly profitable products.

Fast-food milkshakes often contain a cocktail of additives, alongside high-fructose corn syrup and non-milk fat, added to give a sweet creamy flavour. A large strawberry 'shake' from one major chain contains only 1.8 per cent strawberry juice concentrate, backed up with food colouring to make it pink, and 74 grams of sugar; that's 82 per cent of an adult's recommended daily intake, and 25 per cent of an adult's entire daily allowance of calories: far too much for most children to cope with. Monoglycerides and diglycerides help to emulsify the fats and fluids; pectin, gums and gels enrich the texture; and Frankenstein science adds what nature hasn't.

Creating an artificial strawberry flavour might require over 50 different chemicals, according to a *Guardian* newspaper report. Now, reproducing anything that resembles the complex flavour of ripe, fresh fruit must take extraordinary skills in chemistry, but for me it's madness, when we have fresh strawberries at hand to make the most superb milkshake. Perhaps it's about profit more than quality, when we might not know the long-term health implications of every ingredient and how they interact with each other.

I believe with all my heart that children have the right to grow up healthy and happy, and that it's never too soon for them to start learning about the food choices they will have to make as adults. Making your own milkshakes is more than just delighting your kids with something delicious and natural – it is an active political statement. It teaches your children that they are in control of their own food, and making something together is also an opportunity to educate our children about the war waged on them in the drive for profit.

MAKES ≈ 800ml

For a malted chocolate milkshake
8 scoops of vanilla ice cream
4 tablespoons cocoa powder
4 tablespoons barley malt extract

For a strawberry milkshake
8 scoops of vanilla ice cream
200g ripe hulled strawberries, halved
1 small banana, peeled and sliced

For a vanilla milkshake
8 scoops of vanilla ice cream
½–1 teaspoon vanilla extract

To make any of these milkshakes, just whizz all the ingredients together in a blender and serve immediately in a tall, chilled glass (I like to put mine in the freezer for 30 minutes). If you like a thinner milkshake, just add a dash of ice cold milk to adjust the thickness, once all the ingredients are smooth.

RETURN TO THE WILD ORGANIC GREEN ICED TEA

The importance of organic farming relates as much to the land and the creatures in, on and above it, as it does to the benefits which might accrue to us as consumers, knowing that we're buying something free of pesticides. To understand more about how growing tea organically can benefit the entire local ecosystem, I visited an estate which has switched to organic, outside Ooty (Ootacamund) in the Nilgiris District of Tamil Nadu, in southern India.

Within hours of getting off a plane at Bangalore, I am holding my breath as I watch a herd of wild buffalo walk across the tea plantation. I move slowly, trying to get close enough to photograph the bull; he gazes at me, working out if I am a threat to his females, before deciding that I am of no interest. This herd has returned to the estate after 20 years – confirmation of the hard work and dedication, not just to producing really delicious tea, but doing so in harmony with the land.

Being British, I am a dedicated tea drinker. It is the lifeblood of our nation; we connect over tea. We put the kettle on to celebrate and we put the kettle on to commiserate, but the traditional black tea with milk and perhaps sugar is fast being caught up by the interest in green tea. It is repudiated to be healthier, full of antioxidants, and lighter in flavour than black tea, and consumers who are thinking about all aspects of what they drink are increasingly demanding that their tea be organic too.

Here is the way I was taught to prepare iced green tea at the plantation in India, using organic fair trade tea. I've become quite addicted to its fragrance and slightly sweet flavour.

SERVES » 4

2–3 unbleached green teabags
1 tablespoon sugar or light honey
    (optional)
a handful of fresh lemony herbs, such
    as lemon verbena, lemon balm or
    lemon thyme
ice cubes, to serve

Boil the kettle and pour a generous cupful of the water into a large teapot, to warm it. Let it stand: it's best if the boiled water cools slightly, ideally to 93°C if you have a thermometer handy. Empty the teapot, drop the teabags in along with the sugar or honey, if you like. Pour 1 litre of just-boiled water over, put the lid on and brew for 3 minutes. Remove the teabags so that the tea doesn't stew, and leave to cool completely.

To serve, put the herbs and some ice cubes into a large jug and pour the tea over.

PACKAGING-FREE LEMONADE ICE LOLLIES

You'll think I'm crazy, but I was seen peering into the bin next to the little kiosk in a local park one sunny afternoon. It was full of the brightest, most colourful packaging you could imagine from the frozen lollies people had been enjoying. Over the following days though, I thought about the contents of the bin and my children licking their melting ice lollies with those garish wrappers, and I began to wonder about food packaging materials. What kind of inks were used? What were those shiny wrappers made of? What kind of glue stuck the edges together? How did they get the wrappers to be so thin and flexible? Was the packaging biodegradable?

One report by Dr Jane Muncke and a team at the Food Packaging Forum Foundation in 2014, suggested that more than 170 potentially dangerous chemicals are legally used in the production of food packaging. Substances such as phthalates are routinely used to increase the flexibility, transparency, durability and longevity of food packaging, and while the Food Standards Agency states that these toxic ingredients in packaging are at safe levels, the report suggested that 'food contact materials are one possible source of food contamination because chemicals may migrate from the material into the food'. More to the point: because the chemicals are in the packaging and not the food, the manufacturers don't even have to declare them on the labelling, so we as consumers are not helped towards making informed decisions. And even if we could, I don't know if enough work has been done on testing the rate at which chemicals may leach from packaging into food, or if those substances are bioaccumulative (built up within the body at a faster rate than they can be removed by excretion or decay).

I won't be a spoilsport and suggest our children never have an ice lolly from a shop, but there's a huge pleasure in making your own, with the reassurance that you know exactly what's in them. They look pretty, cost a fraction of the price, save on packaging, are made from fair trade ingredients and you can buy moulds which are free from phthalates and BPA (bisphenol A). The recipe below is the children's version, but add a good glug of gin and they become adult XXX-rated. Just a word of advice... don't mix the two versions up!

MAKES *10-12

zest and juice of 7 unwaxed lemons
500ml cold water
500g caster sugar
5 sprigs of lemon thyme
2 bay leaves
To freeze
slices of cucumber and mint leaves or
   edible flowers such as pansies,
   lavender or borage

Put all the ingredients in a heavy-based saucepan and bring to the boil. Reduce the heat and simmer for at least 5–6 minutes until the sugar is fully dissolved. Strain and leave to cool before transferring to a jug. Covered and chilled, this should keep in the fridge for 3–4 weeks.

To make the ice lollies, dilute the lemonade slightly with cold water; it should taste much sweeter than you would drink it at room temperature, as the sensation of sweetness is reduced when frozen. Put slices of cucumber, mint leaves or edible flowers inside the moulds. Fill with the diluted lemonade, then freeze for 4–5 hours.

FAIR TRANSPORT SUMMER RUM COCKTAIL

'We are now exactly inside the hurricane, in the eye of the storm, where there is a storm all around us, and only innovative people will survive.' Captain Arjen van der Veen, fair transport pioneer and one of the three captains of the Tres Hombres speaking about climate change

Global climate change has already had measurable effects on our environment. Glaciers have shrunk, ice on rivers and lakes across the world is breaking up much earlier each spring, and plants and animals have been affected, even displaced. Trees are flowering earlier and crops in some places are struggling because of drought, while in other parts of the world, changing weather patterns have brought more rain. Soil erosion and changes in the climate will mean that there is less land for cultivation, and our farming patterns have simply not adapted to changing circumstances. It will mean 'climate refugees' as people move in search of food and water, and almost inevitably, conflict, hunger and death.

We have to wake up fast and start acting now. Getting the world to change has been compared to turning a supertanker around, but we have the technology and the information to do it. We now have, according to leading scientists, about a decade left in which to change course. Using a supertanker as a metaphor brings me to one of the ways we can effect change: the way in which our food is transported.

Much of our food is carried on cargo vessels, but apparently just 16 of the world's largest ships produce as much sulphur pollution as all the world's cars. Gigantic ships need massive engines, and each one can burn as much fuel as a small power station. There is however no effective independent regulation of the shipping industry's pollution record, and supertankers often burn the cheapest, dirtiest fuel available. This contains many hundreds of times the amounts of sulphur permitted in car fuel, pumped into the atmosphere as microscopic, lung-damaging particles, along with as much CO_2 as the global aviation industry produces. In effect, we are giving shipping a licence to pollute.

How can we change this? By acting in a more mindful and considered way. There are three things we can all do immediately: think twice, before buying imported goods we really don't need; buy more of our food and other goods from local producers; and when buying things that just cannot be sourced from nearby, to choose the ones which have been grown or made, and then transported, without causing unnecessary damage to the planet.

The rum I use for making this cocktail was transported from the Caribbean on an old-fashioned sailing ship, with nothing more than the wind to power her. If you're unable to buy something like that, at least look for a fair trade or fair transport label. The syrup itself is made with fresh angelica from my garden, not the crystallised candied sort sometimes used in baking.

SERVES » 4

25cm stem of angelica
2 medium stems of rhubarb
approx. 400g granulated sugar
rum, to serve

Chop the angelica and rhubarb into 3cm lengths, and place in a medium pan. Add about 600ml cold water and bring to the boil. Simmer until the liquid has reduced by about one third and then leave to cool overnight, covered.

Strain and measure the liquid. Depending on the juiciness of your rhubarb, it should be about 400ml. Match the volume in ml with an equal weight of sugar in grams, bring to the boil and then simmer until reduced almost by half, to leave about 500ml of syrup. Skim any scum from the top and cool before straining into a sterilised bottle (see page 184). Keep in the fridge.

Shake 1 part rum with 2 parts syrup and serve over ice (even prettier if edible flowers like pesticide-free lavender, rosemary, borage or rose petals are frozen into the cubes). To make this into a long drink, top with another 4 parts lemonade.

AVOID THE CHEMICALS SUMMER FRUIT SYRUP

Sweet, fruity and deliciously thirst-quenching, fruit squashes are enjoyed by both adults and children alike. The supermarkets dedicate entire sections to juice-based drinks, but it is so easy to make your own, and in doing so you avoid preservatives like sulphur dioxide, high levels of added sugar, glucose-fructose syrup or artificial sweeteners, food colourings and other additives. Honestly, I don't want to buy something labelled 'no added sugar' only to find that instead, it contains sucralose and acesulfame K, and I don't feel reassured when I read that a bottle of fruit and barley squash contains 'glycerol esters of wood rosins'.

Because berries are such a high-value crop, farmers often use pesticides routinely to prevent pest damage, rather than wait and only treat a problem if it happens. Some pesticides can interact with each other, which might increase their toxicity – known as the 'cocktail effect', and the possible long-term effects from the repeated ingestion of low doses of pesticides, fungicides and insecticides are still unknown. There are over 120 artificial chemicals that can be used by fruit farmers in the UK, and according to a report in *The Ecologist* in 2011, some of them like Mancozeb (a fungicide used to control leaf spot, rust and mildew on berries), Cypermethrin (an insectide used on grapes) and Pirimicarb (an insecticide used to kill aphids), have been described as potentially carcinogenic or as environmental toxins.

When I cook soft fruit, I don't want to concentrate any chemical residue on them into whatever I am making. So I look for berries from farmers who use organic methods, and I would encourage you to think about growing your own, if you have space in your garden.

I've been making this recipe for years, and I don't just stick to summer berries. I've used rhubarb and plums successfully too; but the one thing I do ensure is that the fruit is pesticide-, fungicide- and herbicide-free.

MAKES » 1 LITRE

1kg fresh, frozen or home-grown berries
3 star anise
125ml cold water
450g granulated sugar

Wash and rinse the glass bottles this syrup will be stored in, and leave them to dry, then put them in a roasting tin and place in the oven at 170°C/150°C fan/gas 3 for 15 minutes to sterilise them. Wash the tops well in hot soapy water, rinse and leave to dry.

Put the fruit and star anise into a heavy-based saucepan. Add the water, cover and heat slowly until the liquid boils, making sure the fruit doesn't catch and burn onto the base of the pan. Boil for 5 minutes then leave to cool for 15 minutes. Mash the fruit well into the liquid to extract all the flavour, then strain the liquid into a separate pan through a sieve, pressing it firmly against the wire mesh with the back of a spoon to squeeze out every drop. Discard the fruit pulp and star anise.

Return the pan to the heat and stir in the sugar. Bring to the boil for 2 minutes, stirring to help the sugar dissolve. Remove immediately from the heat and leave to cool for 10 minutes. Meanwhile, remove the bottles from the oven and keep warm. Fill the bottles with the syrup, using a funnel and a ladle or a clean, warmed jug. Seal immediately then leave to cool. The syrup will keep for six to eight weeks in the fridge.

CERTIFIED GINGER SYRUP

With its rich, deep perfume, ginger is one of my favourite spices: complex and simultaneously earthy and scented. This dark ginger syrup is for grown-ups. It is both fiery and sweet, makes a wonderful long cold drink cut with lemonade and is equally delicious drizzled over a bowl of vanilla ice cream, but my favourite way to enjoy it is on a cold night with whisky.

The northeast region of India is emerging as a 'hub' for the production of organic root ginger, where it has for many years been an important cash crop for small farmers, accounting for 72 per cent of India's ginger production. The farmers are predominantly from ethnic minority tribal peoples, and women play an important part in the cultivation of ginger, often taking on much of the planting, manuring and harvesting. But most of all, in states like Meghalaya, Mizoram and Nagaland, they have the task of taking it to market and securing an income for their families.

However, it can be a challenging crop to grow in some places, according to a 2013 study of micro-enterprise ginger farming by the United Nations Development Programme. A fungal infection called rhizome rot causes the root to shrivel and the leaves to yellow and dry out, and can affect the entire crop. There is a safe treatment that uses a beneficial fungus (*Trichoderma harzianum*), to parasitise the problem fungi and destroy them, but not all products used in the growing of ginger are safe, or even legal. In 2013, there was a report in the *South China Morning Post* of farmers in China's Shandong province overusing a highly toxic pesticide called Aldicarb, which was never approved for use in ginger cultivation. But how do we prevent or discourage unscrupulous or uninformed farmers from using these pesticides?

One of the most powerful means of change is education: showing how to adopt the traditional and sustainable methods used by tribal farmers in north-east India, or how to use permitted agrochemicals in a safe and effective manner. We can support this by buying organic, fair trade or other certified produce, that helps farmers on the ground work safely and effectively.

MAKES » 750ml–1 LITRE

350g fresh root ginger, peeled and
    chopped
1 litre cold water
1kg soft brown sugar
250g muscovado sugar

Put the ginger into a large pan with the water, bring to the boil and simmer until the ginger is soft. Leave the ginger and liquid to cool, then liquidise in a blender until smooth. Strain through a muslin cloth back into the saucepan, discarding any fibre left behind, then add the sugars and dissolve over a low heat. Bring the syrup to the boil and simmer until reduced by half. The syrup should just coat the back of a spoon. Be careful not to over-reduce the syrup, or it will become too sticky and toffee-like.

Cool and decant into sterilised glass bottles (see page 184). Depending on how much water has evaporated, and how fibrous the ginger is, you will end up with between 750ml and 1 litre of syrup.

DIG FOR VICTORY RHUBARB AND GINGER GIN

A 'proper' gin and tonic is the drink to appreciate life and celebrate good things with, as well as a reward at the end of a busy day. This fragrant pink 'gin' uses a simple recipe that infuses vodka (as a neutral, unflavoured spirit) with some of the aromatic fair trade spices typically found in gin, ginger from Asia and rhubarb from my garden. It is as delicious as it is pretty.

My rhubarb patch started with a clump from my husband's grandmother's garden. She had got it from her mother, during World War II when the British government asked every family who had a garden to grow some of their own food. This campaign was known as Dig for Victory, and food rationing was so strict that householders needed little encouragement to make this domestic contribution to the war effort.

The 'war' we are facing now is one of climate change, with the expectation not just of higher average temperatures but also of extreme weather events such as drought, coastal flooding and cold waves becoming more common, and these climatic changes will challenge global food production. A 2014 report by the Intergovernmental Panel on Climate Change said that 'all aspects of food security are potentially affected by climate change'. As growth in crop yields, particularly wheat, is slowing, there are fears that food production will be unable to keep up with the needs of our planet's growing population.

So again, we are back to us, as individuals, taking small steps. We can dig for victory again and grow some of our own food, in gardens or even window boxes and containers. Rhubarb is just one example of a 'backyard' crop that is low maintenance, wonderfully versatile, good to eat and which, as this recipe shows, has other uses.

MAKES » 800ml

700ml gin or vodka
400g rhubarb, chopped, leaves
   discarded
5cm slice of fresh root ginger
100g caster sugar
2 tablespoons juniper berries
1 tablespoon fennel seeds
1 whole nutmeg
4 cardamom pods
a few black peppercorns
1 vanilla pod

Put all the ingredients into a 2-litre jar or bottle, stir well, then seal tightly and leave on a sunny windowsill. Over the next week the alcohol will infuse with the spices and turn gently pink. Give the jar a regular stir (or shake, if sealed tightly) to dissolve the sugar. You can add more sugar to taste, but I prefer some tartness.

To serve, strain the pink gin over crushed ice and top with tonic water and a slice of lime or lemon.

DIY UNBLEACHED HERB TEAS

I had never considered the colour of teabags until it was pointed out to me that some brands do not use bleached paper. A side-by-side comparison showed the bleached one was really white, compared to the pale sepia colour of the unbleached bag. In truth, the teas made by each bag had no discernible difference in taste. It was simply a matter of the white one appealing to some idea of purity. But what was the price of that unsullied appearance?

To get that whiteness, the teabag paper is usually treated with chlorine dioxide, which bleaches the natural beige colour (though there is a chlorine-free bleaching process where oxygen, ozone or hydrogen peroxide are used instead). The paper may then be treated with a potential toxin called epichlorohydrin, to strengthen the paper and stop it tearing so easily.

Depending on what chemicals are used, the process can release toxic by-products, harmful to both the environment and human health. Environmental protection agencies across the world have rules that limit the amount of air- and water-pollution caused by the bleaching process, but environmentalists claim that waste water contaminated by these harmful chemicals is nevertheless often discharged into local waterways, contaminating fish and wildlife, and entering the food chain through farmland and food crops.

It's a completely unnecessary chemical process simply for aesthetic reasons, and I have to note the craziness of making white bleached teabags when our intention is often to make dark brown tea! If we cared more about the planet than about the colour of our teabags, there would be fewer chemicals contaminating our air and water, and in the end the tea tastes just the same, whatever the shade of the teabag.

We have choices: we can buy ethically produced tea, loose or in unbleached bags, or we can get creative and make our own herb teas, using all sorts of unsprayed, unwaxed, pesticide- and chemical-free ingredients, such as dried rose petals, cinnamon, juniper berries, vanilla or dried orange and lemon peel, and herbs like bay leaves, rosemary, bergamot, lemon verbena or lemon thyme. You can make herb teas as strong or as weak as you like; here are some of my favourites.

MAKES 4 CUPS

For garden herb tea
1 sprig of fresh rosemary
a small handful of fresh oregano
1 small bay leaf
1 teaspoon light runny honey

For zesty organic ginger tea
3 x 10cm stems of fresh lemon balm
4 sprigs of lemon thyme
1 teaspoon dark honey
7.5cm piece of fresh root of ginger, sliced
    very finely

For lemon verbena tea
a large handful of lemon verbena
1 teaspoon light brown sugar

For winter spice tea
1 star anise
2 cinnamon sticks
5cm piece of fresh root ginger, thinly sliced
2 cardamom pods, crushed
zest of 1 orange, peeled off in long shreds
1 tablespoon muscovado sugar

To make any of these teas, first warm the pot with some boiling water, let it stand for a few minutes, then empty the water. Add the tea ingredients, top up with fresh boiling water and leave to infuse for:

Garden herb tea: 4 minutes

Zesty organic ginger tea: 5 minutes

Lemon verbena tea: 3–4 minutes

Winter spice tea: 5–6 minutes (this is my standby if I am warding off a cold: sometimes with an added glug of brandy).

BASICS

RIGHT FROM SCRATCH SOURDOUGH STARTER

A sourdough starter is a mixture of flour, water, yeast and bacteria that will help to give your bread an extraordinary flavour and texture. There are various ways of creating a starter but before you begin, it is worth considering what you are doing: getting the wild yeasts already present in both the flour you use and in the air around you to multiply so that you can use them in baking. It can be a real challenge, and establishing a healthy culture can take a little time.

To be honest, for people who are completely new to sourdough I might suggest that obtaining an established starter from a friend is easier than making your own, especially if you have no experience with sourdough; and it's essential if you want to bake bread straight away. An established starter is more reliable, as the yeasts and bacteria have been active over a period of time and make it stable and more dependable. However, there is something exceptionally satisfying about creating your own sourdough starter. You need just two ingredients – wholemeal flour and water – together with some basic equipment and conditions.

These are the conditions necessary to make a sourdough starter:

» Start with a warm room. Not hot, not cold, just a room that is pleasant to be in.
» A non-reactive container to make and store your starter in (sourdough starter is acidic and will react with certain metals). I prefer old-fashioned stoneware pots to store my starter in, but a glass bowl is fine too.

» A fork or whisk to incorporate air.
» A breathable lid or cover, such as a clean tea towel.
» A space to catch your wild yeast with no other cultured foods nearby (or there may be a crossover and you might not get the yeast you need).

Put 200g wholemeal flour and 200ml filtered water at 28°C in a large jar, then whisk vigorously and cover with a breathable lid. Set aside in a warm place for 24 hours.

You must then feed your starter. Remove and discard a large cupful of the mixture. Add ½ cup of flour and ½ cup of filtered water and stir well. Cover and set aside for a further 12–24 hours. Soon you might be lucky enough to see some bubbles, which indicate that oragnisms are present, but even if you don't, just keep going. Refresh your starter daily for 10–14 days (fewer in warmer weather), discarding half the starter before every feed.

After about 10–14 days your sourdough starter should be beautifully bubbly and should have enough yeast and bacteria to be active enough to bake with. Once it is established, keep it in the fridge and feed it about once every 2 weeks. On rare occasions you may make your own starter only to find that it smells or tastes absolutely horrid or that the bread and other baked goods it produces isn't all that pleasant. This means that the bacteria that has occupied your starter is not the right kind, and the lactic acid (which is what makes the starter inhospitable to other organisms) hasn't got going. You will need

to discard this one and start over and move the location of your culture to a different room.

I most often find that people who are having difficulties have meddled with the process. You need to be patient. You do not need hot water, live yeast, grapes, rhubarb or any other additions to get yeast going. It is naturally present in the grain that you use and for the best results, use stoneground organic wholemeal flour that has not been treated with fungicide or with pesticides as the stoneground roller milling process has a lower temperature and so the yeasts survive the milling process.

The process of making sourdough bread

Bread is at the absolute heart of eating in the most sustainable way possible and out of all the recipes in this book this is the one with the most potential to transform your everyday meals.

I have always known the aroma of freshly baked bread. For me, it represents home, family, warmth and love. My earliest memories are of sitting at the table, spreading cold salted butter on Irish soda bread, baked by my mother on the farm we grew up on in the 1970s. When I was nine my parents bought a house in Nadaillac, a small village in south-west France. It had been empty for many years, without a bathroom or heating, but they lovingly restored it and we spent every holiday there. We were known as 'Les Anglais'. My bedroom in the attic had pigeonholes, and every morning at 3am I'd be woken by wafts of woodsmoke from the bakery just 30 yards away. It didn't take me long to follow the smoke in the air and every morning by the age of eleven I was creeping past my parents' bedroom and running down the alleyway and across the square to the bakery. I'm not sure how much help I was to the baker, but he was amused by my English accent and enthusiasm. He'd drink black coffee, smoke Gauloises and allow me to sweep up and serve customers. One day he gave me a piece of dough to shape and bake and it was there that I fell in love with bread making, as he taught me the simple rhythm of baking. I'd return in the early light to my parents with a freshly baked loaf of warm Pain de Campagne, with its rugged crust and soft chewy interior. We'd eat my bread with sun-warmed tomatoes from a friend's working garden, a can of pâté, cheese from Madame Boukier and rough red wine, all grown and made in the village by the people who I'd served in the bakery earlier that morning. I felt connected.

Now I teach people to bake sourdough bread, how to find their local miller and how to bake with organic flour, and I encourage everyone to eat bread with the best seasonal local produce. Life can be chaotic but there is great pleasure in simple things. This recipe is my attempt to make the world a better place by showing people how to make and bake a great sourdough loaf that encapsulates so many answers to the food issues that challenge us. It's a joy for me to see good bread become part of someone's everyday life. The simple truth is that baking sourdough

bread will help you to eat ethically and sustainably: by baking your own bread with a sourdough starter fed by locally grown organic flour, you'll supports local farmers and the environment.

Water

Just use tap water, it's free and by far the most sustainable option. Though there is often chlorine as a gas added to it, you can leave water to stand in a jug before using so the gas escapes. Don't use bottled water – the distance it travels and the bottling process aren't environmentally sound. Water from your tap at home is the way to go.

Flour

The key terms I look for when choosing flour to bake with are organic, local and heritage. The flour I use is grown locally, farmed using organic principles without pesticides, herbicides or external fertilisers, and this helps to sustain the fragile ecosystem of our environment.

At the same time many organic growers now plant a mixture of wheat varieties to increase crop diversity, as some varieties will prosper when others fail if there are changes in environmental conditions. The heritage grain specialist John Letts is of the opinion that blending hundreds of different genetically diverse varieties at least guarantees a partial yield and could help to build crop resilience, because when one variety fails due to a virus or lack of rain, another will survive.

Often heritage grain varieties have been collected from plants which were grown on

marginal land and they are therefore more likely to survive a drought. They might have longer and more extensive root systems, which means they can seek out moisture and micronutrients from deep in the soil – up to a metre or more down – and some believe that the flour is more nutritious a result. This is aided by the mycorrhiza, the microscopic fungi that live inside the plants' roots, which facilitate access to these trace minerals.

Salt

Salt for me is an integral part of a sourdough loaf, primarily as a flavour enhancer. I once accidentally made a batch of sourdough without salt, then when I toasted a slice and took a bite, I was horrified. For me, salt makes bread taste great. Yes, we have a problem with high levels of salt in supermarket ready meals, relying on its flavour-enhancing properties to compensate for cheap ingredients, but in an artisan loaf a little salt is a fair addition. Some salts also have a unique mineral content and these trace minerals are believed to help with our day-to-day biological functions. One of my food heroes, Mark Bitterman, author of *Salted*, points out that salt has the unique power to temper unwanted flavours such as excessive bitterness or sweetness.

For me, sourdough bread made with flour that is local, organic and heritage deserves salt that reflects those ingredients' values. For example, using salt harvested by small producers, like Halen Môn from Anglesey, means that you help support another artisan producer.

FUNDAMENTAL SOURDOUGH__**The most sustainable bread in the world.** Wild yeast starter (*opposite*). Mixing ingredients (*Top*). Lifting and folding the dough and shaping it ready to put into a banneton (*Bottom*).

FUNDAMENTAL SOURDOUGH The most sustainable bread in the world

So here's my recipe for sourdough, and for me it's the one recipe that my kitchen life happily revolves around. It produces a loaf with a crisp, crackling crust, an extraordinary aroma in the crumb, and when sliced and served it's the thing that will get you the most praise. My family loves it, my friends are always impressed when I place the loaf on the table, and my hope is that it will be a recipe that brings you the pleasure it brings me. And most importantly, it's the cornerstone for me in sustainable and ethical living. It helps to support local farmers and millers, and it avoids using commercial yeast where the production relies on petrochemical by-products. You nurture the starter at home, you make it slowly so the flavour is as rich as it can be, and with your hands and simple ingredients you craft a beautiful loaf of sourdough bread.

MAKES ▸ 1x1.85kg LOAF

Recommended equipment
1.5kg round banneton
baking dome
grignette, for slashing the dough
For the sourdough
650g water at exactly 28°C
200g levain, refreshed using equal parts
    flour to water, and mixed 8 hours
    before you are ready to bake*
    (see below)
1kg stoneground organic white flour,
    plus extra for dusting
20g fine sea salt
organic polenta flour, for dusting

* Levain is made by taking 20g starter and adding 90ml cold water and 90g strong white organic flour. Leave covered with a damp cloth on the counter for 6–8 hours; you will see that is it bubbly and ready to use.

Mix (at about 6pm):

In a large bowl, whisk the water and levain together. Add the flour and salt (combined well) and mix until all the flour has made contact with the water and there is no more dry flour. Do not knead.

1st ferment:

Cover the bowl with a clean, damp cloth and leave the dough to rest in a cool environment for 30 minutes. This is called autolyse.

Fold (6:30pm):

Lift and fold the dough over on itself. Do a quarter turn of your bowl and repeat three more times. Over the next hour lift and fold your dough again twice.

Shape (7:30pm):

Shape the dough lightly and place into a dusted banneton. Dust with white flour and cover with a damp tea towel. Leave to prove in the fridge for 8 hours.

Bake (8am):

The following morning, preheat the oven to 220°C/200°C fan/gas 7 for at least 30 minutes before you are ready to bake with your baking dome in the oven. The dome must be very hot. Take the dome out of the oven and sprinkle a little polenta flour over the bottom. Put the dough into the dome and slash the top of the bread using a grignette (or lame), then place the lid back on top and return to the oven as quickly as possible. Bake for 45 minutes then reduce the heat to 190°C/170°C fan/gas 5 and bake for a further 30 minutes. Finally remove the lid and bake for another 10 minutes.

You can judge how dark you like your crust, but I suggest that you bake it until you have a dark brown crust for a really authentic loaf. Sourdough is best left to cool completely before slicing and is even better if left for a day to let the full flavour develop. Once the bread is completely cool, store in a linen or cotton bread bag or folded tea towel. If you don't like a crunchy crust, then wrap the bread in a clean tea towel while it is still warm.

NO PACKAGING YOGURT

UK government statistics suggest we produced 10.65 million tonnes of packaging waste in 2012, and recycled just over 61 per cent of it. Even when we recycle such a considerable amount of our packaging, I wonder if we could do without most of it. Often it's used once, then promptly discarded, in a rush from the factory to shop, to fridge, to landfill or recycling plant: with little thought of the impact on the environment the whole process makes.

Having once collected yogurt pots for a children's project, it occurred to me as I looked at the pile of containers, with their silver lids, bright inks and marketing slogans that making my own yogurt wouldn't just reduce this waste but might completely eliminate it.

Making your own yogurt doesn't just eliminate the packaging: it also avoids you consuming a wide range of additives, including modified starches, fructose, artificial flavourings, colouring and sweeteners found in many commercially produced yogurts. The truth is it's ridiculously simple to make your own yogurt, and because it is live, it contains lactic acid bacteria helpful to your digestive system. You don't need artificial anything for it to taste good. My recipe produces a rich and creamy set yogurt with a light acidic tang. Serve with a spoonful of honey, a dollop of jam or just as it is – natural and not a plastic pot in sight.

SERVES » 6

1 litre whole milk
6 tablespoons organic live plain
   whole-milk yogurt

Pour the milk into a saucepan and put the pan over a low heat. Stir gently, watching it carefully, until the temperature reaches 91°C, which is just below boiling point. Then remove from the heat and leave until the temperature falls to 46°C.

Pour the milk into a warm sterilised bowl. Whisk in the live yogurt and the bacteria will start to work on the fresh milk and convert it into yogurt.

Cover the bowl with a clean tea towel and place it somewhere warm overnight. An airing cupboard or a shelf above a radiator is fine, or alternatively, you can pour it into a warmed, wide-mouthed Thermos flask and seal.

If the yogurt is still runny in the morning, leave it wrapped up in the warm for another couple of hours. When it is the right thickness, transfer it to a sterilised container with a lid and store in the fridge; a Kilner jar is ideal. Homemade yogurt is not as thick as commercially produced yogurt, so to get a thicker Greek-style set, strain it through a muslin-lined sieve over a bowl for a few hours.

The yogurt will keep for up to two weeks in the fridge and you can use some of it to make your next batch.

BACK GARDEN BLACKCURRANT JAM

As a baker I am slightly obsessed with the things that go on my bread. For me it has to be the very best butter, the most delicious cheese or the fruitiest, loveliest of jams. There are a few good commercial jams, but homemade is still undoubtedly the best. If you are lucky enough to have space in your garden, then a blackcurrant bush will give you sustainable fruit to make jam with. The variety called 'Ebony' is ideal for small gardens as it takes up little space planted against walls and fences, while 'Big Ben' will yield up to 4.5kg of fruit each year from a single bush. You can buy one of these modern heavy cropping plants for the same price as four pots of supermarket jam, and the bushes could live for up to 50 years. That's 225kg of fruit over a lifetime, which according to my recipe below, will provide you with 750 pots of jam.

This recipe also works with gooseberries, raspberries, redcurrants and blackberries, but I have chosen to use blackcurrants because they make the most fabulously intense jam with a wonderful knobbly texture, which is a delight smothered over hot buttered toast. I prefer a dollop of blackcurrant jam to raspberry in my rice pudding, it makes a wonderful topping for cheesecake, is sublime stirred into porridge with a whisper of cream, and it goes a treat with freshly baked scones.

Making jam is simple and requires minimal effort for maximum results, but I do have one piece of advice, and that is to ensure that your fruit is cooked well before adding the sugar. If you add the sugar too early on in the cooking process it makes the blackcurrants hard.

MAKES » 5 x 450g JARS

1.5kg blackcurrants
2 star anise
100ml cold water
1kg jam sugar
juice of 1 lemon

Preheat the oven to 170°C/150°C fan/gas 3 and put the clean, empty jars (but not the lids) into the oven. Pop a small saucer in the fridge to chill, so you can test the setting point later.

Put the blackcurrants, star anise and water in a large saucepan, cover and heat gently for about 10–12 minutes. Gently stir occasionally and keep the pan covered. Once the blackcurrants are cooked and the consistency is half juice and half fruit, stir in the sugar and lemon juice. When the sugar dissolves, bring the jam to the boil for 4–5 minutes on a good bubble. As the jam boils, use a metal spoon to skim off any froth appearing on the top, but take care not to remove too much of the jam with it.

Once the jam reaches setting point it should be viscous enough to coat the back of a metal spoon. To test for setting point, remove the pan from the heat and drop about 1 teaspoon of jam onto the cold saucer from the fridge. Leave it for about 1 minute. If it is ready, then the jam will wrinkle as you run a spoon through the centre. If it doesn't wrinkle, return the pan to the boil and repeat this process about 2 minutes later. Do take care not to over-boil the jam. This setting point should really take no longer than 7–10 minutes at most to achieve.

Once the jam has reached the setting point, take the pan off the heat, remove the jars from the oven and ladle the jam into them using a jam funnel and a clean, dry tea towel to protect your hand from the incredibly hot bubbling sugary mixture. After a minute or so, taking care not to burn yourself, screw the clean lids on; the heat from the jam will ensure that the lids are sterilised. Label and date the jars (the idea isn't to have an old, unidentified jar sitting at the back of your cupboard!).

FOOD CHAIN APPLE AND ROSE HIP CHUTNEY

It is worth a moment's consideration that when you forage for rose hips – the firm orange pods left after the flower has bloomed on the stem – you become a part of the woodland's fragile ecosystem. Every hip you pick would have been a source of food for insects, animals and birds, so if you take too much it has a knock-on effect for the whole food chain. It is easy to overestimate the amount of hips you need when you are picking in hedgerows, so try to work out what 500g of hips look like before you go out. Weigh a handful as a simple guide.

MAKES » 4x450g JARS

500g rose hips, topped, tailed and
    seeds removed
600ml white wine vinegar
500g cooking apples
seeds from 4 cardamom pods
200g dried sour cherries
7.5cm piece of fresh root ginger, peeled
    and finely grated
400g soft brown sugar
juice of 1 lemon
zest of 2 unwaxed limes

Wash and drain the rose hips, then put them in a bowl with the vinegar and leave overnight.

The following day, peel, core and roughly chop the apples and grind the cardamom seeds into a powder with a pestle and mortar. Put all the ingredients into a large, heavy-based saucepan and slowly bring the mixture to a boil, stirring to prevent it catching on the bottom of the pan. Boil for 5 minutes then reduce the heat and simmer, still stirring at regular intervals, until the mixture is thick and gloopy and sticks to the back of a spoon. To test the set, put a small plate or saucer into the fridge to chill, then pour a teaspoon of the chutney onto it and let it briefly cool. If the syrup wrinkles when you poke it with a finger it's ready, otherwise let it reduce further and cook a little more, then test again.

Preheat the oven to 170°C/150°C fan/gas 3. Put the clean, empty jars (not the lids) on a baking tray and put them in the oven until hot to sterilise them.

Remove the jars from the oven. Leave to cool for about 2 minutes then carefully ladle the bubbling chutney into the hot jars using a jam funnel and a clean, dry tea towel to protect your hand as you hold the jars steady and fill them. Put on the clean lids straight away; the heat from the chutney will ensure the lids are sterilised. Be careful not to burn yourself.

FORAGER'S CRAB APPLE JELLY

You don't have to buy everything. Some foods are free and fallen crab apples are one of those things that are too often overlooked. Poached with sugar, then mashed and strained, the resulting jelly has the most glorious colour, richly perfumed, with a flavour that's sweet and refreshingly tart.

Before you assume that crab apples are only found wild in the countryside, I can tell you that they actually grow wherever their seeds are dropped by birds. Some of the very best trees can be found in urban areas, next to roads, in parks, on scrubland, along canal towpaths, and in other people's gardens. Just don't pick the fruit without making sure that it's alright for you to take it.

I can't bear to watch fruit rotting. So if I spot fruit lying on the ground under trees in other people's gardens I will knock on the door and offer to do a fruit-for-jam swap. You don't need loads, just a carrier bag full, and I've made so many new friends this way.

MAKES » 1.5 LITRES approx.

1kg crab apples
approx. 1.3 litres water
900g white sugar

Rinse and roughly chop the crab apples, throwing away any stalks or leaves, and put them in a large pan with the water. Bring to the boil and simmer over a gentle heat. Cover and stir occasionally until the fruit is soft. Leave the mixture to cool, then mash up the apples. Let the mashed apples and liquid strain slowly into a clean pan (ideally, overnight), through a large sieve lined with either a clean cotton tea towel or a piece of muslin.

Once the straining is finished, preheat the oven to 170°C/150°C fan/gas 3 and put a small saucer into the fridge so you can test the set later on. Put the clean, empty jars (but not the lids) on a baking tray and pop them into the oven.

Discard the pulp left in the sieve, measure the strained crab apple liquid, and weigh out an equal quantity of sugar (e.g. 900g of sugar to 900ml of apple juice). Pour the liquid into a large, heavy-based pan, add the sugar and heat slowly until the sugar dissolves. Then cook the jelly for 8–10 minutes on a rolling bubble, stirring occasionally. As the jelly boils, use a metal spoon to scoop off any foam, as this improves the clarity of the jelly when set (there should be no more than half a mug of froth).

When the jelly coats the back of a metal spoon, it's ready to test for setting point. The easiest way I know is the wrinkle test. Remove the pan from the heat while you test, and put a spoonful of jelly onto the cold saucer from the fridge. After a minute or so the jelly should be cold and it will wrinkle a little as you run your finger through it. If not, simply return the saucepan to the boil and repeat this test in another 2–3 minutes.

Remove the jars from the oven. Ladle the jelly into the now sterilised jars while still hot, using a jelly funnel and a dry tea towel to protect your hand. Put the clean lids on straight away; the heat from the jelly will sterilise them. Take care not to burn yourself.

FREE-RANGE EGG LEMON CURD

Yellow as a pot of sunshine: who can resist lemon curd? When you make it, the whole kitchen smells of citrus and the reward is a sweet, sharp preserve to spread on warm toast, or my favourite, sourdough crumpets.

The eggs you use do matter. When the long-awaited ban on eggs from battery-caged chickens came into force in early 2012 there was a cheer let out by hundreds of food and animal activists. It was a happy egg day. But shoppers still faced an ethical choice when buying eggs, because the ban didn't really mean the end of cages: just battery cages. The new 'enriched' cages are better than what they replaced, but they still confine the birds and limit their natural behaviours such as dust bathing, wing movement, walking, socialising, perching and nesting. So what about barn eggs? The name sounds romantic, conjuring an image of a traditional wooden farm building in a field, but make no mistake: these poor girls do not have access to the outside either and never see the sun. This is sadness itself. Denying any creature daylight and natural movement is inhumane and abhorrent.

The simplest thing you can do to make an ethical egg choice is either to keep your own chickens or buy eggs from free-range hens that have access to outdoor space. So when you enjoy your pot of lemon curd, you know that the hens that laid the eggs enjoyed a little sunshine too.

MAKES » 2x450g JARS

200g unsalted butter
4 sprigs of fresh thyme (I like to use
    lemon thyme)
zest and juice of 4 unwaxed lemons
400g white granulated sugar
4 large eggs, at room temperature
pinch of sea salt

Put the butter and thyme into a medium bowl set over a pan of simmering water. Do not let the bottom of the bowl touch the water. Add the lemon zest, juice and sugar. Stir occasionally until the butter has melted, then remove the pan from the heat and leave for 10 minutes so the thyme infuses the butter mixture.

Remove the herbs and return the pan to the heat, so the water simmers again under the bowl. Whisk the eggs in a separate bowl, then reduce the heat under the butter mixture and gradually beat the eggs into it.

Return the water under the bowl to a simmer and stir the mixture regularly for about 10 minutes until the curd is thick and custard-like in consistency. Then turn off the heat, remove the bowl from the pan and stir the lemon curd as it cools to prevent a skin forming. Pour into two sterilised jars (see page 200) and seal. It will keep for two weeks in the fridge.

FAIR AND SIMPLE SHORTCRUST PASTRY

Shortcrust pastry is so versatile. It is the base for pies, pasties and tarts. You can, of course, simply buy ready-made pastry, but by making your own you can be sure of using local butter, organic eggs, fair trade sugar and sea salt. Plus it gives you the chance to use organic heritage or heirloom (as they are known in the US) wheat varieties. These grains often make quite 'soft' flour, which makes the pastry tender and delicate, and older wheat varieties are often grown in a more environmentally friendly way without fertilisers and they're really flavoursome. Many heritage flours are wholemeal, so check first and if yours is, you'll need to sift it through a fine sieve to remove the bran before using it. As stoneground heritage flours can also absorb water differently, be prepared to slightly adjust the amount of liquid you add when making the pastry.

By far the easiest way to make shortcrust pastry is to use a food processor. Do not worry if you don't have one because the principles are exactly the same working by hand, except you must try to remember that the colder your hands and the quicker you work the mixture, the less you will warm the fat, which helps keep the pastry light and short.

SAVOURY SHORTCRUST PASTRY

225g plain white flour (I often use heritage flour,
    such as Rivet or spelt), plus extra for dusting
pinch of salt
50g cold butter, diced
50g cold lard, diced
1 egg yolk
2–4 tablespoons cold water

Put the flour, salt, butter and lard in the bowl of a food processor, and pulse until the mixture resembles fine breadcrumbs. Then add the egg yolk and 1–2 tablespoons of water, and pulse to bring the mixture together. Add more water, just 1 tablespoon at a time if necessary, to get the right consistency and pulse again, but do not keep mixing or it will make your pastry tough. Just before you feel the mix has come together, tip the mixture onto a very lightly floured surface and knead it together with your hands. You will find your hands a better judge than your eyes. If necessary add a tiny last drop of water if the dough still feels crumbly, then lightly shape. Wrap in greaseproof paper and place in the fridge to chill for 20 minutes before using.

SWEET SHORTCRUST PASTRY

225g plain white flour (again, a heritage variety if
    you can find one), plus extra for dusting
pinch of salt
50g vanilla-infused fair trade sugar
100g cold butter, diced
1 egg yolk
2–4 tablespoons cold water

The method for this is exactly the same as above, adding the sugar to the flour, salt and butter.

RESPECTFUL CHICKEN STOCK

The aroma of fresh stock bubbling away on the stove is comforting to many, and reassuring. It's the promise of a good meal to come.

As a teenager I was both a vegetarian, and a member of an animal rights group. Even as I left that stage of my life, it was a shocking thought to be boiling the bones and carcasses of birds, and initially I was deeply uncomfortable with it. I spent a lot of time considering what it was to eat another creature and since then, I've questioned and formed principles which, twenty-five years later, are still with me.

I came to the conclusion that I would reduce the amount of meat I ate, and then only consume meat I knew to have been reared and slaughtered with consideration for the animal's wellbeing. But also I would recognise the sacrifice made, by using every part of the bird or animal, as a mark of respect. Those principles hold firmer than ever, and the extra effort to find, cook and pay for a fairly treated bird, and then making stock from the carcass, makes both financial and moral sense.

There is no particular strict ingredients list. Making chicken stock is about using up leftover chicken bones, with herbs and vegetables, so if you have less-than-fresh or imperfect vegetables, then great. Use them. Save the stems of parsley and rosemary and freeze your chicken carcasses one at a time until you have enough. There is no need to defrost. They can be used straight from the freezer.

You need a large stockpot; mine is an old cast-iron round casserole that holds about 6.5 litres. Depending on what you want to use the stock for, you can add spices: black pepper, a couple of cardamom pods, a clove or two or one star anise. You can add salt at the end to taste, as it may be easier to judge the amount once the stock is reduced.

MAKES ▸ 750ml approx.

1kg roasted chicken carcasses (I like to add in some raw chicken wings if I don't have enough bones)

1kg peeled and roughly chopped assorted vegetables, such as carrots, celery, onions, leeks or peppers

small bunch of parsley

2 bay leaves

couple of sprigs of thyme

salt

Put the chicken, vegetables and herbs into a large stockpot with enough cold water to cover (about 2 litres). Bring to the boil and very gently simmer for 2–3 hours, topping the pot up with water every so often so that the bones stay covered. During this time you need to use a large metal spoon to skim and discard any scum that forms. After this time, strain the stock, discarding the bones and vegetables.

Return the stock to the pan and reduce it by half or more by simmering for longer – this makes it both more concentrated and easier to store. Season with a little salt if necessary. Once cold, store in the fridge for up to a week in a jar with a lid, or freeze until required.

HOMEMADE FREE-RANGE RAPESEED MAYONNAISE

When I look out over the fields near my home in early spring there is a sea of intense yellow. You can hear bees buzzing, as farmers have planted rapeseed, and the vivid colour tells you it's in full bloom. Many farms across Europe now grow it for the production of cold-pressed rapeseed oil, as opposed to the high-temperature process used by big vegetable oil refiners, which also used solvents and other chemicals to bleach and deodorise the oil. Cold-pressed, it has a distinctive flavour, making it a serious alternative to olive oil as it has lower levels of saturated fats and higher levels of omega-3 and omega-6 fatty acids. The perfect partner to free-range egg yolks from my own chickens.

Here in this mayonnaise, the rapeseed oil gives a delicate nutty flavour that is delicious served with salads or poached vegetables. If you have a stick blender this recipe is even easier, but I have made this just using a balloon whisk. It's hard work but then I feel I can justify the calories I consume. I like to add more flavours, sometimes: right at the end you could mix in a mashed clove of garlic, or a small bunch of fresh tarragon, neatly chopped, or 1–2 teaspoons of fair trade smoked paprika. Think of this as a perfect 'base' recipe and add the flavours that suit your meal.

MAKES » 2x350g JARS

3 egg yolks
1 tablespoon Dijon mustard
2 tablespoons apple vinegar or the juice
    of ½ lemon
pinch of sea salt
approx. 600ml rapeseed oil

Put the egg yolks into a large bowl. Add the mustard, vinegar, salt and a glug of oil (about 3 tablespoons).

Beat for about 10 seconds, then add another glug of oil and whisk again. Repeat this, adding the oil gradually, until the mayonnaise has a good, glossy emulsified look to it, and a thick consistency. Don't worry if it's too thick, as you can thin it by adding a little more lemon juice. At this point you can divide the mayonnaise between separate bowls and make two or even three batches, adding different herbs or spices to each one, as desired.

ETHICAL SALAD DRESSINGS

Talk to any farmer in the world and it seems they have the same goals: grow their crop, get a fair price and live a productive life on land they love, but getting a fair price is not always straightforward when the product that you grow is a commodity and prices are dictated by both demand and market forces. I spent some time with the managing director of Pelia olive oil, based in Greece, who explained that the business started as a result of frustration that local small-scale olive farmers would be forced to sell premium, hand-harvested olives at very low prices no matter how good the olives. It broke their hearts to know that their harvests ended up being blended in with thousands of gallons of oil destined for big brand names.

In buying small olive oil directly from small olive growers' cooperatives or through choosing to buy fair trade oil we can help support farmers. Fair trade oil is, in many cases, the more expensive option, and some fair trade oils can be more than twice the price of a comparable organic, extra virgin oil from Italy, but around the world there are many other small independent producers of fantastic quality olive oil that are well worth supporting.

I often choose fair trade Palestinian olive oil, as olives are an important part of Palestine's agricultural economy and paying a fair price really does make a difference to their income. I also use a fresh, green and vibrant oil produced by a Greek producer, who goes above and beyond to pay local olive farmers a premium which actively discourages the farmers from yielding to the power of large corporations wanting bulk oil cheaply. Many fairly traded olive oil producers bottle locally and employ village labour so the money stays in the community, which in our troubled economic times is a lifeline to those farmers. I've also noticed that fairly traded olive oil tends to be the cold-press method of extracting oil, which yields wonderful quality oil with very little oxidisation. Buying cold-pressed extra virgin olive oil also avoids using oil derived from industrial processes that extract the last of the oil from the first pressing by using a mixture of high heat and chemical solvents to extract any remaining oil. Personally, I'd far sooner spend a little more, use a little less, support farmers and completely avoid any chemical extraction whatsoever.

These two dressings are my staples, perhaps because they reflect my duel Italian/French heritage. They are incredibly simple to make. Try the French dressing over cold cooked green beans or over fresh sun-ripened chopped tomatoes, or the Italian dressing over a chunky green garden salad.

ITALIAN DRESSING

100ml olive oil

35ml apple vinegar

2 tablespoons very finely grated hard
    sheep's cheese

1 teaspoon honey

½ garlic clove, very finely chopped

generous pinch of sea salt

freshly ground black pepper

FRENCH DRESSING

100ml olive oil

35ml white wine vinegar

1 large garlic clove, very finely chopped

1 teaspoon Dijon mustard

generous pinch of sea salt

white pepper, to season

This is the simplest of recipes. In either case, put all the ingredients in a jam jar, screw the lid on tightly and shake vigorously. These will keep stored in the fridge for two weeks.

THREE FLAVOURS OF SALT

Salt is essential to life. Our muscles and organs need it to function and yet salt is demonised in the media. Excessive consumption of it is blamed for high blood pressure and increased risk of strokes, and in mass-produced ready meals it appears to be used indiscriminately with fat and sugar to increase the flavour.

There are three main kinds of salt you can buy: standard table salt, sea or river salt, and unrefined rock salt, but within these categories there are many variations.

Refined table salt, the cheapest of the three, contains none of the trace elements often found in sea or rock salt. It is simply sodium chloride, processed to whiten it and stripped of other minerals, mixed with an anti-caking agent like sodium ferrocyanide. Sea or river salt is made by evaporating sea or river water until only the salt remains; and rock salt is mined from salt deposits in the earth. Both sea or river salt and rock salt are usually sold unrefined and without additives. Alison Lea-Wilson, who founded the Welsh sea salt company Halen Môn together with her husband David, told me that these unrefined salts are usually off-white, grey or even pink in colour: like the silvery 'Sel Gris de Guerande' coloured by the pans in which it crystallises, or the multicoloured shades of rose in Himalayan rock salt or Murray River salt. Alison says that the minerals these salts contain give it a fresh taste and sparkling appearance, whereas table salt has a flat and sometimes bitter aftertaste, possibly due to the anti-caking agent.

I've been blending salt with other ingredients at home for over twenty years to make flavoured salt: from using a dried vanilla pod added to a pot of salt through to ground cocoa nibs mixed with large crystal salt. But my favourite way is just using herbs and dried chillies from the garden. These salts are best used within 4–6 months.

ROSEMARY AND ORGANIC LEMON SALT

5 tablespoons coarse sea salt
3–4 tablespoons fresh rosemary leaves
    (discard the stems)
zest of 1–2 lemons

There is something entirely romantic about making this particular recipe by hand. Perhaps it is the smell of the rosemary, combined with the lemon, which makes me think of the south of France. Simply chop the ingredients up as small as possible and then, using a pestle and mortar, grind them together until they are fully combined.

If you are making lots or are in a hurry, then combine all the ingredients in a food processor and pulse until they are a similar size and well combined.

Spread the mixture out on a baking tray or a piece of baking parchment and allow to air-dry for two days, turning the mixture occasionally to make sure it dries evenly. You can also 'heat-dry' in the oven at 65°C for 2 hours, stirring frequently. Once the salt is dry, store it in a non-metallic airtight container.

INDIAN SPICED SALT

2 tablespoons dried mixed ground spices:
    a mixture of cumin, coriander, cinnamon
    and star anise, fennel or aniseed
4 tablespoons sea salt

Mix and bottle.

DRIED AND SMOKED PAPRIKA SALT

3 large dried whole chillies
1 heaped tablespoon smoked paprika
4 heaped tablespoons fine sea salt

Mix and bottle.

A RECIPE FOR SUSTAINABLE BOTTLED WATER

Something like 800 million people do not have access to clean water, and almost 2.5 billion don't have adequate sanitation. I've watched children collecting canisters of water before they go to school, and it's both sobering and humiliating to see that and then consider what we so often take for granted. There are places in the world where bottled water might seem desirable. It is not, however, necessary in the West. It is also, in my opinion, totally insane to buy water to quench your thirst in a disposable plastic bottle if you live in a country where you have access to clean tap water.

It is estimated that over 80 per cent of all single-use water bottles simply get thrown away when empty. These plastic bottles used for water take over 1,000 years to biodegrade and produce toxic fumes if incinerated. So usually, they simply go to landfill.

Buying bottled water is not only up to 2,000 times more expensive than a glass of tap water; if you buy bottled, you are actively wasting resources and exacerbating climate change. With transport the fastest-growing source of greenhouse gas emissions, it makes no sense to have bottled water travelling hundreds, if not thousands, of miles.

On an even more sombre note, the bottled water industry is also implicated in the abuse of scarce resources in developing countries, where some of the biggest global players are pushing to privatise and control public water resources for their own profit. Deep wells drilled for their bottling factories can dry up traditional water sources used by local communities, or lead to them becoming chronically polluted. Safe water then becomes both a privilege and a marketable commodity, and the bottled water companies then sell back to people the thing they had previously been able to take for granted: drinking water. The chairman of one multinational food and drink company is on record as saying that the idea that people should have access to water as a basic human right is 'an extreme solution', but do we really believe that water should be turned into a privatised, branded foodstuff, like a chocolate bar or a soft drink?

We can decide not to be part of this process by buying one robust and almost endlessly reusable water bottle, and filling it with the clean and reliable tap water we have immediate access to. If you are one of those people who hates the taste of chlorine (as I do) you can add a piece of activated charcoal which is also know as Binchotan charcoal. It has been made in the Kishu region of Japan since the Edo period (17th–late 19th century) and is used for its purification virtues. It is made by steam-activating oak over a long period of time before raising temperatures up to 1,000°C. Its porous surface has a huge array of cavities creating a massive surface area, which can suck up a whole host of undesirable substances that stick to it. This makes it an effective filter and water purifier while also releasing natural minerals. You can 'refresh' charcoal by boiling it in a saucepan of 650ml water for ten minutes, which releases any captured chemicals. Discard the water and then leave the sticks to dry in the window in sunlight. Generally I refresh mine every 2–3 weeks, and keep a stick going daily for about six months. You can then simply dispose of it in the compost. Two 10cm sticks of charcoal will filter 1.5 litres of water over 4–5 hours. Once you have used the water, simply refill your container.

MAKES ▸ 1 BOTTLE

Equipment
reusable bottle
For the water
tap water
activated charcoal, if required

Fill the bottle with water. Add the charcoal. Screw the top on and leave in the fridge for 8 hours before drinking.

Repeat for up to six months, before changing the charcoal.

"Enough. Man is capable of reform once presented with the facts, and the fact is that bottling water and shipping it is a big waste of fuel, so stop already. The water that comes to your house through a pipe is good enough, and maybe better."

RESOURCES

These are not just resources, these are a list of the companies and people who I connected with as I was researching and writing this book.

INGREDIENTS AND EQUIPMENT

www.bakerybits.co.uk – For heritage and organic flour, sourdough starter and bread-making equipment.

www.barfoots.com – For sweet potatoes grown with love.

www.black-blum.com – For activated charcoal/Binchotan charcoal sticks and portable water bottles.

www.britishquinoa.co.uk and **www.hodmedods.co.uk** – For quinoa.

www.cabritogoatmeat.co.uk – For goat meat.

www.ciderbrandy.co.uk – For British brandy.

www.chocolatiers.co.uk and **www.originalbeans.com** – For amazing sustainable chocolate.

www.clipper-teas.com – For tea it just has to be Clipper. They go above and beyond to makes sure their tea is ethically and sustainably produced and delicious.

www.cocoarunners.com and **www.rocococholates.com** – Stock The Grenada Chocolate Company chocolate.

www.commonfarmflowers.com – Flowers that are not from your own garden can be bought from my lovely friend Georgie.

www.davidaustinroses.co.uk – All the roses I grow in the garden are from David Austin Roses.

www.dovesfarm.co.uk – For a range of organic flour.

www.fleurfields.co.uk – Wine from my mum and dad!

www.froothie.co.uk – My blender takes a hammering so I have a powerful blender that is great for soups and milkshakes, which has a safety mechanism to stop over-enthusiastic people like me breaking the engine!

www.halenmon.com – For the most beautiful sea salt.

www.hampshirecheeses.co.uk – For Tunworth cheese.

www.hodmedods.co.uk – For beans.

www.herbcentre.co.uk and **www.jekkasherbfarm.com** – The herbs in my garden are mostly from inspirational Jekka and from the Herb Centre.

www.Ndali.net – Vanilla from Lulu Sturdy's fair trade farmers in Uganda.

www.nealsyarddairy.co.uk – For Tunworth and a range of cheeses.

www.newdawntraders.com – For fair transport rum.

www.pelia.co.uk – For olive oil.

www.smithymushrooms.co.uk – For a range of delicious mushrooms.

www.therealboar.co.uk – Boar meat and salami.

www.thompson-morgan.com – All my vegetable seeds are from here and they stock a wonderful selection of heritage seeds too.

www.waterbuffalo.co.uk and **www.laverstokepark.co.uk** – For buffalo milk and meat.

JOURNALISTS

This book could not have been written without the work of the following journalists. They are inspirational, brave and write without compromise. Their work is too long to list here but these are their twitter handles so please do get your devices out and connect.

BBC Radio 4 Food Programme @BBCFoodProg – Investigating every aspect of the food we eat, produced by @DanSaladinoUK and presented by @SheilaDillon.

Mark Bitterman @Selmelier – Saltman extraordinaire who will change the way you look at salt forever.

Joanna Blythman @JoannaBlythman – If you follow one person, make it journalist and author Joanna Blythman. She writes without compromise, uncovering the truth about our food system.

Damian Carrington @dpcarrington – Head of environment at the Guardian.

Felicity Carus @FelicityCarus – Specialises in energy matters.

Charles Clover @CRHClover – Author of *The End of the Line*.

Louise Gray @loubgray – Former *Telegraph* environmental correspondent. An ethical

carnivore.

Philip Lymbery @philip_ciwf – Author of *Farmageddon: The True Cost of Cheap Meat* and Chief Executive of Compassion in World Farming (CIWF).

Jonathon Porritt @jonathonporritt – Author and broadcaster focusing on palm oil and clean energy.

Lucy Siegle @lucysiegle – *Guardian* journalist.

Tristram Stuart @TristramStuart – Author of *Waste: Uncovering the Global food Scandal*.

Bee Wilson @KitchenBee – Journalist and author.

BOOKS

Confessions of an Eco Sinner: Travels to find where my stuff comes from – Fred Pearce (Eden Project Books)

Eight Steps to Happiness – Geshe Kelsang Gyatso (www.kadampa.org)

Share: The cookbook that celebrates our common humanity – edited by Alison Oakervee (Kyle Books)

TWITTER

I'm on Twitter and Instagram @VanessaKimbell. Yes it is really me and I do respond, as do lots of twitter climate and food activists. Look them up, follow them, interact and join in. It is a movement that more and more people add their voice to every day.

Good hashtags are #climatechange

#Sustainable #Sourdough #Environment

@CarlLegge – Food activist and author of *The Permaculture Kitchen*.

@chantalcoady – Founder of Rococo Chocolates.

@DanBarber – Author of *The Third Plate* and well worth reading.

@earthhour – Ways to use #YourPower and change climate change.

@fergustheforage – Wild food specialist.

@LucyGilliam – Eco sea queen and environmentalist. Founder of eXXpedition (@eXXpedition) exposing unseen plastics in the ocean.

@MrJunkFoodChef – Founder of @RealJunkfood, an organic network of #PAYF cafes worldwide, intercepting food 'waste' to create healthy meals.

@realbread – Campaign for real bread with just flour, salt, water and yeast.

@SusFoodTrust – A brilliant site on sustainable food and farming.

@TRESHOMBRESRUM – #Fairtransport rum.

WEBSITES

There are many websites reporting on environmental issues, but perhaps my favourite site, which I have found myself on many times during the research of this book is the Guardian environmental page which can be found at **www.theguardian.com/uk/environment**

Other good sites include:

www.antislavery.org – Reporting and campaigning on slave labour and people trafficking.

www.ciwf.org.uk – Compassion in World Farming website and a must read for any omnivore.

www.foodtank.com – Addressing ethical food issues globally.

www.forkedmagazine.org – Hard-hitting food journalism, investigations, ideas and all things ethical and culinary.

www.msc.org – Marine Stewardship Council website and a useful source of information on sustainable fish.

www.soilassociation.org – A great place to find out more about organic food.

www.sourdough.co.uk – My website about baking with sourdough and wild yeast.

www.sustainablefoodtrust.org – Brilliant articles on sustainable food, farming and related issues.

www.theecologist.org – A global site tackling environmental issues worldwide.

INDEX

ACKNOWLEDGEMENTS

Each and every page in this book is a testament to the time, effort, advice, kindness and encouragement of some very special people. In the beginning Lulu Study of Ndali Vanilla opened her world to me and opened my eyes. Thank you to Kato Bernard for showing me around. My thanks to Chantal Coady of Rococo chocolates, an inspiring friend who introduced me to Mott Green and encouraged me to investigate the world of chocolate.

To my friend Xanthe Clay, I cannot thank you enough for those moments that you helped me to understand what I wanted to do, and made me believe I could do it. To Patrick Thornberry, of BakeryBits, who has supported and encouraged me and whose ethical principles translate into the core of his business. Thank you to my agent Michael Alcock, for waiting patiently for me to deliver my proposal and introducing me to Kyle Cathie. A huge thanks to Kyle, who saw my vision for this book, shaped my thoughts and enabled it to be written.

Thank you Diana Henry for your generosity and introducing me to the wonderful dream team: Joss Herd, Laura Edwards, Rachel Wood and Tabitha Hawkins, who did the styling, photographs, props. Thank you all for the beautiful photographs and your warmth, friendship and talent that bring the recipes to life. (And Rachel Wood and Ian Wright – thank you for keeping me sane!) A titanic thank you to Andrea Barbu, my assistant. Jane Humphrey, I love the design. It combines the stories and the recipes beautifully, and in such a straightforward way that it captures the message of food activism as part of our everyday lives perfectly – thank you.

Thank you to my remarkable editor Vicky Orchard, for your constant care and the freedom to just write, and to my dear friend and mentor, the brilliant David Whitehouse, thank you for your copy-editing. You are a genius.

To my eco sister, Dr Lucy Gilliam, whose advice pointing me towards the environmental issues where we can make the most difference can be spotted through out the book.

Arjen van der Veen, captain of the Tres Hombres who challenged me not just to talk about how to change things, but to be the change that empowers people to make a difference. Here it is Arjen.

Dan Saladino is my real life hero (the producer of the programmes that change the politics and the landscape of the food world every week) – thank you for including my reports as I researched ingredients for this book on BBC Radio 4's *Food Programme*. It has been amazing to hear the voices of the farmers I have written about on the programme, which has been inspiring me to my core for as long as I can remember. Thank you to Sheila Dillon, whose uncompromising style and ethical drive has been an inspiration to me, thank you with all my heart for the foreword.

To the producers who supplied ingredients: John Dorrian of Smithy Mushrooms Ltd, Stacey Hedges of Hampshire Cheeses Ltd for the Tunworth cheese, Nick Saltmarsh, managing director of Hodmedod Ltd for the local organic beans. Barfoots of Botley Ltd, for providing the sweet potatoes and information on the Senegalese project for the sweet potato soup. Julie Rush and Colin Randel, vegetable product managers at Thompson and Morgan Seeds for the beautiful plants I grew for this book. Thank you to Jekka McVicar for the herbs and advice, and the fabulous Georgie Newbury of Common Farm Flowers for her guidance on flowers. And to Carl Legge for providing the nasturtium seeds.Three cheers to my sister-in-law, Melissa Kimbell, and Ben and Sophie Kimbell and Serenity Simon – for being my unexpected guests.

To the Clipper Tea team, thank you for taking me to India and for sharing your values and total commitment to the workers and environment. To Rob Bates at the Grenada Tourist Board. To The True Blue Bay Resort, the Calabash and to Aubrey at Ndali Lodge in Uganda, thank you for the accommodation. To my dad, thank you for accommodating my food obsession in Vietnam and to my mum for helping me with my own young family while I work.

To my family, my sister Fleur and my friends, for allowing me to disappear not just around the world, but into my study too, and being there as I resurface. To my children, Libiana, William and Isobel for encouraging me, and telling me how proud they are as I missed events to write this. Thank you. To Polly (my Jack Russell), for being my constant companion sitting under my desk as I wrote.

To my husband, my all, for your unwavering support, thank you doesn't even begin to cover it. You are my foundation.